"An excellent, politically neutral look at the scriptures that guide great leaders. Winder gives an illuminating synopsis of the leaders behind the quotes. It's refreshing to read about America's leaders in a politically unbiased format."

—Michael Conklin, author of *Inaugural Addresses Examined*

"In this informative and inspiring volume, Mike Winder takes us into the souls of great men and women to look at the holy words that give light to their feet and purpose to their march. Perhaps in their driving inspirations you can find inspiration of your own."

—Bob Lonsberry, award-winning columnist and talk-show host

"Mike Winder's collection usefully illustrates not only the profound impact religion has had on American culture and politics, but also the diverse ways in which Americans have understood what it means to be religious in the first place."

—Matthew Bowman, author of *Christian: The Politics of a Word in America*

"The core of any individual is their chosen beliefs; and nothing speaks louder than when a person shares their favorite scripture from Holy Writ. Winder gives us this revealing window to the soul of America's leaders and the key to their motivation and actions."

—Ronald L. Fox, author, historian, and advanceman
for six presidents of the United States

FAVORITE
SCRIPTURES
of
100
AMERICAN
LEADERS

Mike Winder

PLAIN SIGHT
PUBLISHING

An imprint of Cedar Fort, Inc.
Springville, Utah

ISBN 13: 978-1-4621-2313-1

Published by Plain Sight Publishing, an imprint of Cedar Fort, Inc.
2373 W. 700 S., Springville, UT 84663
Distributed by Cedar Fort, Inc., www.cedarfort.com

LIBRARY OF CONGRESS CATALOGING-IN-PUBLICATION DATA

Names: Winder, Michael Kent, author.
Title: Favorite scriptures of 100 American leaders / Michael Winder.
Description: Springville, UT : Plain Sight Publishing, an imprint of Cedar
   Fort, Inc., [2019] | Includes bibliographical references.
Identifiers: LCCN 2018042777 (print) | LCCN 2018047424 (ebook) | ISBN
   9781462129850 (epub, pdf, mobi) | ISBN 9781462123131 (perfect bound : alk.
   paper)
Subjects: LCSH: Bible--Quotations. | Sacred books--Quotations. | Civic
   leaders--United States--Biography. | LCGFT: Quotations. | Biographies.
Classification: LCC BS416 (ebook) | LCC BS416 .W56 2019 (print) | DDC
   220.5/2--dc23
LC record available at https://lccn.loc.gov/2018042777

Cover design by Jeff Harvey
Cover design © 2019 Cedar Fort, Inc.
Edited and typeset by Nicole Terry and Kaitlin Barwick

Printed in the United States of America

10 9 8 7 6 5 4 3 2 1

Printed on acid-free paper

To my sweet Karyn, in celebrating twenty years of bringing
me happiness, joy, and four beautiful children.

"Let thy fountain be blessed: and rejoice with the wife of thy youth."
—*Proverbs 5:18 (King James Version of the Bible)*

Contents

All scripture is given by inspiration of God, and is profitable for doctrine, for reproof, for correction, for instruction in righteousness:

That the man of God may be perfect, throughly furnished unto all good works.

—2 Timothy 3:16–17 (King James Version of the Bible)

Prologue

During the depths of the Civil War, Mary Lincoln's personal seamstress, Elizabeth Keckley, recalled a careworn President Lincoln visiting with his wife. When Mary asked him if there were any updates from the War Department, he replied, "Yes, plenty of news, but no good news. It is dark, dark everywhere."

So what did Abraham Lincoln do during such a trying time? Keckley reports that he "reached forth one of his long arms and took a small Bible from a stand near the head of the sofa, opened the pages of the holy book, and soon was absorbed in reading them."

She says that the president was immersed with reading the Bible for a quarter of an hour and recalls, "The face of the president seemed more cheerful. The dejected look was gone, and the countenance was lighted up with new resolution and hope. The change was marked that I could not but wonder at it."

She later learned that he was reading the comforting pages of Job. "He read with Christian eagerness," she said, "and the courage and hope that he derived from the inspired pages made him a new man." Keckler, a former slave and God-fearing Christian herself, marveled at the sight: "What a sublime picture was this! A ruler of a mighty nation going to the pages of the Bible with simple Christian earnestness for comfort and courage, and finding both in the darkest hours of a nation's calamity. Ponder it, O ye scoffers of God's Holy Word, and then hang your heads for very shame!"[1]

America's leaders have long relied on the holy word of scripture to guide them and bring comfort. For many, the verses that soothe their souls and inspire their hearts come from the Bible, but in an increasingly diverse nation, leaders are also drawing wisdom from the Qur'an, the Torah, Hindu and Buddhist texts, the Book of Mormon, and more. May you also be inspired by the divine word and the journeys of faith as shared by our past and current presidents and leaders.

NOTE

1. Elizabeth Keckley, *Behind the Scenes: Thirty Years a Slave, and Four Years in the White House* (New York: G. W. Carleton & Co., 1868), 118–19. h/t Kristine Frederickson.

1

JOHN ADAMS

Second President of the United States

Adore God's Power, Wisdom, and Works

God is one, creator of all, universal sphere, without beginning, without end. God governs all the creation by a general providence, resulting from his eternal designs. Search not the essence and the nature of the Eternal, who is one; your research will be vain and presumptuous. It is enough, that, day by day and night by night, you adore his power, his wisdom, and his goodness, in his works.

—Introduction to the Shasta (five-thousand-year-old
Hindu scripture translated from Sanskrit)

America's second president and first vice president valued the Old and New Testaments. In 1813, he wrote to Thomas Jefferson in a Christmas letter, "I have examined all, as well as my narrow sphere, my straitened means, and my busy life would allow me; and the result is, that the Bible is the best book in the world."

In the same letter, he also acknowledged his inspiration from the Hindu scriptures, specifically quoting the above passage from the Shasta. He explained, "Where is to be found theology more orthodox, or philosophy more profound, than in the introduction to the Shasta?"

It was not difficult for John Adams to connect the beautiful truths he found in the Bible with the scriptures of the Eastern religions. "The fundamental principle of all philosophy and all Christianity is, 'Rejoice always in all things.'"[1]

Consistent with this belief, in another letter to Jefferson, he penned, "The love of God and His creation, delight, joy, triumph, exultation in my own existence . . . are my religion."[2]

NOTES

1. John Adams, "Letter from John Adams to Thomas Jefferson," *Beliefnet*, retrieved 4 Apr 2017, http://www.beliefnet.com/resourcelib/docs/72/Letter_from_John_Adams_to_Thomas_Jefferson_1.html.
2. Lester J. Cappon, ed., *Adams-Jefferson Letters* (Chapel Hill: University of North Carolina Press, 1975), 369.

2

JOHN QUINCY ADAMS

Sixth President of the United States

Trust in God's Protection

Except the Lord build the house, they labour in vain that build it: except the Lord keep the city, the watchman waketh but in vain.

—Psalm 127:1 (King James Version of the Bible)

Our sixth president quoted this verse of the Psalms in his inaugural address. "Knowing that," he said about the verse, "with fervent supplications for His favor, to His overruling providence I commit with humble but fearless confidence my own fate and the future destinies of my country."[1]

The second President Adams loved the Holy Scriptures. "I have made it a practice for several years to read the Bible through in the course of every year," he wrote in his diary in 1848.[2] He was once president of the American Bible Society and said of the Good Book, "When duly read and meditated on, it is of all books in the world, that which contributes most to making men good, wise, and happy."[3]

Adams was optimistic about the missionary fervor of the early 1800s. "Whoever believes in the Divine inspiration of the Holy Scriptures must hope that the religion of Jesus shall prevail throughout the earth," he said.

Adams believed in flooding the world with scripture and prayed that "the associated distribution of the Bible proceed and prosper till the Lord shall have *made bare his holy arm in the eyes of all the nations; and all the ends of the earth shall see the salvation of our God*" (Isaiah 52:10, KJV).[4]

Once, in a letter to his son, George Washington Adams, the sixth president pointed out his daily ritual of reading the Bible. "My custom is, to read four or five Chapters of the Bible, every morning immediately after rising from bed," he wrote. "It employs about an hour of my time."[5]

In this letter, the father instructed that the Bible teaches one how to love their God and their fellow man. He also quoted the New Testament itself in encouraging reading of the Bible. "The first and almost the only book deserving of universal attention is the Bible," Adams said. "I speak as a man of the world . . . and I say to you, *Search the Scriptures*" (John 5:39, KJV).[6]

NOTES

1. JQA's inaugural address, quoted in John C. McCollister, *God and the Oval Office* (Nashville: W Publishing Group, 2005), 33.
2. Ibid, 32.
3. "God in the White House," *PBS*, retrieved 4 Apr 2017, http://www.pbs.org/godinamerica/god-in-the-white-house.
4. W. H. Seward, ed., *Life of John Quincy Adams* (Auburn, NY: Derby, Miller & Company, 1849), 248.
5. JQA in a letter to George Washington Adams, 1 Sept 1811, retrieved 20 Sep 2018, http://religion.s3.amazonaws.com/jqa/John_Quincy_Adams.html.
6. Art Farstad, "The Bible and the Presidents," *Faith Alone Magazine*, retrieved 21 Mar 2017, https://faithalone.org/magazine/y1992/92feb1.html.

3

CHESTER A. ARTHUR

Twenty-First President of the United States

Looking to the Lord for Deliverance

In thee, O Lord, do I put my trust; let me never be ashamed: deliver me in thy righteousness.

Bow down thine ear to me; deliver me speedily: be thou my strong rock, for an house of defence to save me.

—Psalm 31:1–2 (KJV)

When President Garfield eventually died of his bullet wounds, Vice President Chester Arthur prepared to take the oath of office as president. His beloved wife, Nell, a devout Episcopalian, had also passed away the previous year, and she was the greatest religious influence on Arthur.

Nell had a lovely voice and sang in the choir. When the clerk of the Supreme Court, James McKenney, provided Arthur a Bible to be sworn in on, Arthur requested that it be turned to the first two verses in Psalm 31.[1] He said that these verses reminded him of the sweet *Te Deum* that Nell used to sing on Sunday mornings when she was in the choir.

After being sworn in on those verses, the new Republican president declared, "I assume the trust imposed on me by the Constitution, relying for aid on Divine guidance and the virtue, patriotism, and intelligence of the American people."[2]

NOTES

1. "The Swearing in of Chester A. Arthur," Joint Congressional Committee on Inaugural Ceremonies, retrieved 11 Apr 2017, https://www.inaugural.senate.gov/about/past-inaugural-ceremonies/swearing-in-of-vice-president-chester-arthur-after-the-assassination-of-president-james-garfield.
2. John C. McCollister, *God and the Oval Office* (Nashville: W Publishing Group, 2005), 108.

Bible - could relate to All

Psalms (Same verse meant any terms)

4

JOE BIDEN

Vice President of the United States

Blasting Pharisees and Hypocrites

*Alas for you, scribes and Pharisees, you hypocrites! You pay your tithe of
mint and dill and cummin and have neglected the weightier matters of
the Law—justice, mercy, good faith! These you should have practised,
those not neglected.*

You blind guides, straining out gnats and swallowing camels!

*Alas for you, scribes and Pharisees, you hypocrites! You clean
the outside of cup and dish and leave the inside full of extortion and
intemperance.*

*Blind Pharisee! Clean the inside of cup and dish first so that it and
the outside are both clean.*

—Matthew 23:23–26 (The New Jerusalem Bible)

Joe Biden grew up in a middle-class Catholic family in Pennsylvania and
later Delaware. He served as a county councilman in New Castle County,
Delaware, and was elected to the US Senate seven times before serving as the
nation's first Catholic vice president.

"We all practice the same basic faith but different faiths," he said in a 2016 speech. "I happen to be a practicing Catholic, and I grew up learning from the nuns and the priests who taught me what we used to call Catholic social doctrine. But it's not fundamentally different than a doctrine of any of the great confessional faiths. It's what you do to the least among us that you do unto me," he said, quoting Matthew 25:40. "It's we have an obligation to one another. It's we cannot serve ourselves at the expense of others, and that we have a responsibility to future generations."

Biden continued, "All faiths have a version of these teachings, and we all practice and preach that we should practice what we say."[1] Perhaps it is because of this view that he is especially vexed with what he views as hypocrisy in many of the world's religions.

In his 2008 bid for the White House, Biden was asked in a primary debate to name his favorite scripture. "Christ's warning of the Pharisees," he replied, alluding to the firm denouncing of religious hypocrisy found in Matthew 23. "There are many Pharisees, and it's part of what has bankrupted some people's view about religion," Biden said. "And I worry about the Pharisees."[2]

Biden also acknowledged another scripture he likes that is part of his favorite hymn. "My favorite hymn in my church is based on the ninety-first Psalm," he said at the White House Easter Prayer Breakfast. "It's 'On Eagle's Wings.' And it's my wish for all of you. You may remember the refrain. It says: 'He will raise you up on eagle's wings, and bear you on the breath of dawn. Make you to shine like the sun, and hold you in the palm of His hand.'"

Biden is a lifelong man of faith. He once mentioned that his wife, Jill, had recently taped a quote on his bathroom mirror from Danish theologian Søren Kierkegaard that says, "Faith sees best in the dark." The vice president elaborated on this: "All of you know better than anyone that faith is a gift from God. Because faith works best when you're the least. Faith works best when you're most frightened, in my view. And faith works best when you're not exactly sure where to go."[3]

Notes

1. "Joe Biden: 'I Happen to Be a Practicing Catholic,'" *Cybercast News Service,* 30 Mar 2016, http://www.cnsnews.com/news/article/cnsnewscom-staff/joe-biden-i-happen-be-practicing -catholic.
2. Jeff Zeleny, "The Democrats Quote Scripture," *New York Times,* 27 Sep 2007, https:// thecaucus.blogs.nytimes.com/2007/09/27/the-democrats-quote-scripture.
3. "Joe Biden: 'I Happen to Be a Practicing Catholic.'"

5

TERRY BRANSTAD

Governor of Iowa

All Scripture Is Essential

If my people, which are called by my name, shall humble themselves,
and pray, and seek my face, and turn from their wicked ways; then will
I hear from heaven, and will forgive their sin, and will heal their land.

—2 Chronicles 7:14 (KJV)

B ranstad, who was appointed ambassador to China by President Donald
Trump, holds the distinction of the longest-tenured governor in
American history. He was governor of Iowa from 1983 to 1999 and again
from 2011 to 2017.

His mother was Jewish, and his father was Lutheran, which is the faith
Branstad was raised in and where he learned to love the Bible. He later converted to the Roman Catholic Church.[1]

In 2014, Branstad issued a proclamation invoking scripture: "NOW,
THEREFORE, I, Terry E. Branstad, as Governor of the State of Iowa, do
hereby invite all Iowans who choose to join in the thoughtful prayer and

humble repentance according to II Chronicles 7:14 in favor of our state and nation to come together on July 14, 2014."[2]

In 2016, the Republican governor issued another proclamation, declaring, "All Scripture is essential to prepare us to be the people God wants us to be and to accomplish the purpose for which he created us." Branstad also encouraged "all Iowans to join in this historical Iowa 99 County Bible Reading Marathon" and urged "individuals and families in Iowa to read through the Bible on a daily basis each year until the Lord comes."[3]

NOTES

1. Douglas Burns, "Gov: Knocking down commercial property tax a priority in 2012," *Daily Times Herald*, 22 Nov 2011, http://carrollspaper.com/Content/Local-News-Archive/Politics /Article/Gov-Knocking-down-commercial-property-tax-a-priority-in-2012/1/335/13023.
2. Doktor Zoom, "Iowa Was Surely God's Favorite Damn State Yesterday Because Brave Governor Signed Big Damn Prayer Proclamation," *Wonkette*, 15 Jul 2014, http://wonkette .com/554250/iowa-was-surely-gods-favorite-damn-state-yesterday-because-brave-governor -signed-big-damn-prayer-proclamation.
3. Kelly Shackelford and Stephanie N. Phillips, "Branstad's Bible proclamation is sound," *Des Moines Register*, 6 Jun 2016, http://www.desmoinesregister.com/story/opinion/columnists /2016/06/06/branstads-bible-proclamation-sound/85500812/.

6

JERRY BROWN

Governor of California

Where Much Is Given

For unto whomsoever much is given, of him shall be much required:
and to whom men have committed much, of him they will ask the more.

—*Luke 12:48 (KJV)*

Jerry Brown is the son of a California governor and the longest-serving governor of the Golden State. He was the state's thirty-fourth governor, and twenty-eight years later, he was elected California's thirty-ninth governor, giving him the distinction of being both the youngest governor of California since 1863 and the oldest in state history.

Brown is a lifelong Catholic but doesn't like being pinned down too much on his religious beliefs. "What does that mean, by the way?" he replied to a reporter who asked him about being a Catholic. "I'm not a Protestant. And I'm not a communist," he said. "There's a whole train of doctrines and beliefs, and I don't want it to be understood that I'm ready to underwrite everything," he added.[1]

As a boy, Brown graduated from St. Ignatius, a Jesuit high school in the Bay Area. He dropped out of college after a year to attend Sacred Heart Novitiate to prepare to be a Jesuit priest. He was there for three years, until he changed his mind and enrolled in University of California, Berkeley and chose a different path. Years later, he studied Zen Buddhism in Japan, but he at least culturally remained Catholic.

"I think the formation that I've undergone growing up in the Catholic faith, the Catholic religion, puts forth a world that's orderly, that has purpose and that ultimately is a positive," Brown once said in an interview with the *Sacramento Bee*. "And that's very helpful when you look at a world that looks very much the opposite, in terms of the wars, the corruption and the breakdown. And so even though from an intellectual point of view it looks very dark, in another sense I have great faith and confidence that there is a way forward. And I would attribute that in some way to my Catholic upbringing and training."[2]

The Democratic governor doesn't wear his religion on his sleeve, but he did trot out a verse from the New Testament in launching Proposition 30—an ultimately successful ballot initiative to raise the sales tax and income tax on high earners to avoid $6 billion in education cuts.

"It's about taking money from the most blessed and giving it to the schools," he said at the kickoff. "To those who much has been given, much will be required," he continued, quoting Luke 12:48, noting that California's wealthiest "now have an opportunity to give back."[3]

NOTES

1. David Siders, "Jerry Brown, 'Are you Catholic?'" *Sacramento Bee*, 22 Jul 2015, http://www.sacbee.com/news/politics-government/capitol-alert/article28263712.html.
2. Ibid.
3. Anthony York, "Gov. Jerry Brown Formally Kicks Off Prop. 30 Tax Hike Campaign," *Los Angeles Times*, 16 Aug 2012, http://articles.latimes.com/2012/aug/16/local/la-me-brown-taxes-20120816.

7

SHERROD BROWN

US Senator from Ohio

Christian Crusader for Justice

Blessed are the meek: for they shall inherit the earth.

—Matthew 5:5 (KJV)

S herrod Brown, senior senator from Ohio, was raised as a deeply religious Lutheran and taught the importance of studying the Bible. The son of a small-town doctor, he was an Eagle Scout, and his mother instilled in him that because of his comfortable upbringing, "much is expected of [him] for the rest of [his] life." His devotion to the scriptures has remained with him into adulthood. "Sherrod re-read the entire Bible last year," his wife, Connie Schultz, recently pointed out.[1]

"My Lutheran upbringing instructs me and my fellow Christians in the teachings of Jesus to read and follow as best we can the words of the Beatitudes, to try to live our lives and practice our politics as Jesus would have wanted us to," Brown said as a representative on the floor of the US House of Representatives in 2004.

"Every bit of progress in the struggle for economic and social justice is rooted in our Judeo-Christian beliefs," he said in that speech. For example, he said, the fight for expanded health care for seniors and the poor "comes from our understanding of the holy word."[2]

Later in another address, Brown noted that so does advocating for rights for workers and the less fortunate—*the meek*, to use the biblical wording. "We are given the New Testament, which shares with us Christ's teachings of social and economic justice," he said.[3]

Brown believes he is following "the teachings of Christ" when he opposes cuts made in Head Start early childhood programs so that there can be tax cuts for the wealthy. The Democratic senator even claimed, "Our opposition to the death penalty is grounded in the scriptures." He summarized how he uses the messages of scripture this way: "My understanding of the teaching of Christ, my religious upbringing calls me to walk a different path and to express and act upon my faith in the cause of social and economic justice."[4]

NOTES

1. Deidre Shesgreen, "Potential VP Nominee Sen. Sherrod Brown a Staunch Advocate for Workers," *USA Today,* 5 Jun 2016, https://www.usatoday.com/story/news/politics/elections/2016/06/05/potential-vp-nominee-sen-sherrod-brown-ohio/85314668.
2. *Congressional Record—House,* 17 Nov 2004, H9875, https://www.gpo.gov/fdsys/pkg/CREC-2004-11-17/pdf/CREC-2004-11-17-pt1-PgH9875-5.pdf#page=1.
3. Kurt Rand, "Sherrod Brown: Jesus Wanted High Taxes for 'Most Privileged,'" *Breitbart,* 5 Nov 2012, http://www.breitbart.com/big-government/2012/11/05/sherrod-brown-offers-outlandish-perspective-on-religion-and-the-bible.
4. *Congressional Record—House.*

8

SAM BROWNBACK

Governor of Kansas

Child of the Living God

Religion that God our Father accepts as pure and faultless is this: to look after orphans and widows in their distress and to keep oneself from being polluted by the world.

—*James 1:27 (New International Version of the Bible)*

B rownback has been a member of Congress, a senator, and the governor of Kansas, and in 2017 he was appointed by President Donald Trump to be the United States Ambassador-at-Large for International Religious Freedom. He was originally a Methodist, but he converted to Catholicism in 2002 through the conservative Opus Dei order and often attends an evangelical church now, Topeka Bible Church. Brownback claims to be inspired by Mother Teresa's maxim that she loved all religions but was "in love with" her own faith alone.[1]

The Republican has been a champion for religious liberties and outspoken about his faith in God. "I believe that we are created in the image of God for a particular purpose. And I believe that with all my heart," Brownback once said in a debate. "And I'm somebody—I've had cancer in the past. I've had a season to really look at this and study it and think about the end of life. And I am fully convinced there's a God of the universe that loves us very much and was involved in the process. How he did it, I don't know."[2]

In an interview with *Rolling Stone* titled "God's Senator," he repeated his view of our divine nature. "I'm a child of the living God," he said. "You are, too. A beautiful child of the living God." Brownback loves the words of the Bible, and he even built a relationship with Israel Prime Minister Ariel Sharon in which they would study scripture together.

Brownback is passionate about the United States helping in Africa. "We're only five percent of the population," he said, "but we're responsible for thirty percent of the world's economy, thirty-three percent of military spending. We're going to be held accountable for the assets we've been given." When asked about what drives him for such charity, he answered, "Widows and orphans," referencing the New Testament Epistle of James.[3]

NOTES

1. Erasmus, "America's Point-man on Religious Liberty Is Contentious," *Economist*, 30 Jul 2017, https://www.economist.com/blogs/erasmus/2017/07/freedom-s-many-meanings.
2. "Third G.O.P. Debate," *New York Times*, 5 Jun 2017, http://www.nytimes.com/2007/06/05/us/politics/05cnd-transcript.html.
3. Jeff Sharlet, "God's Senator, Who would Jesus vote for? Meet Sam Brownback," *Rolling Stone*, 25 Jan 2006, archived at http://www.kansasprairie.net/kansasprairieblog/?p=11445.

9

GEORGE HERBERT WALKER BUSH

Forty-First President of the United States

Share the Light

Ye are the light of the world. A city that is set on an hill cannot be hid.
Neither do men light a candle, and put it under a bushel, but on a
candlestick; and it giveth light unto all that are in the house.
Let your light so shine before men, that they may see your good
works, and glorify your Father which is in heaven.

—Matthew 5:14–16 (KJV)

The first President Bush was a God-fearing veteran and lifelong
Episcopalian. When accepting the Republican nomination for president, he acknowledged the many volunteers throughout America doing
good, "a brilliant diversity spreads like stars, like a thousand points of light
in a broad and peaceful sky."[1]

When he was sworn in, Bush placed his hand on a family Bible he had opened to Matthew 5, which includes the verses admonishing mankind to perform good works and share their light (quoted above).[2]

"I have spoken of a thousand points of light, of all the community organizations that are spread like stars throughout the nation, doing good," he said moments later in his inaugural address. "I will go to the people and the programs that are the brighter points of light, and I will ask every member of my government to become involved," he said.[3]

NOTES

1. George Bush, "Address Accepting the Presidential Nomination at the Republican National Convention in New Orleans," 18 Aug 1988, in Gerhard Peters and John T. Woolley, *The American Presidency Project*, retrieved 7 May 2017, https://www.presidency.ucsb.edu/documents/address-accepting-the-presidential-nomination-the-republican-national-convention-new.
2. "The 51st Presidential Inauguration," Joint Congressional Committee on Inaugural Ceremonies, retrieved 11 Apr 2017, https://www.inaugural.senate.gov/about/past-inaugural-ceremonies/51st-inaugural-ceremonies.
3. George Bush, "Inaugural Address," 20 Jan 1989, in Bartleby.com, retrieved 7 May 2017, https://www.bartleby.com/124/pres63.html.

10

GEORGE W. BUSH

Forty-Third President of the United States

Mount Up with Wings as Eagles

But they that wait upon the Lord shall renew their strength; they shall mount up with wings as eagles; they shall run, and not be weary; and they shall walk, and not faint.

—Isaiah 40:31 (KJV)

George W. Bush was a born-again Methodist president whose Republican administration was described as "the most resolutely 'faith-based' in modern times."[1] Bush admitted that he read the Bible regularly during his time as president, beginning with his first day in the White House. Don Evans, his Secretary of Commerce, gave him the *One-Year Bible*, which he often used.[2]

During his first inaugural, the weather was stormy and the family Bible he was sworn in on remained closed to protect it. For his second inaugural, on January 20, 2005, "after praying for guidance on the scripture he should choose," wrote his friend Dr. Mike Evans, "he chose a scripture used by

Ronald Reagan at the end of his famous 'Evil Empire' speech at the Twin Towers Hotel" (Isaiah 40:31; quoted above).[3]

The verse perfectly encapsulated Bush's Christian reliability on the Lord and the American symbolism of soaring like eagles. "Think about all that George W. Bush had been through in his first term: 9/11, the assault on America, the wars overseas, so much turmoil and trouble all around," observed Pastor Craig Etheredge, "and yet he chose this verse to say, *If we will wait on God, and if we will look to God, we will mount up with wings as eagles, and the nation will be able to rise above all this. If we focus on the Lord, He will give us the strength; He will give us the courage to walk and not faint.*"[4]

Bush believed literally in waiting on the Lord, like Isaiah instructs. When Bob Woodward in a *60 Minutes* interview asked the president if he consulted with his father, the forty-first president, before declaring war on Iraq, Bush answered, "No. I consulted with a higher Father."[5]

In the memorial service in the National Cathedral after 9/11, President Bush invoked scripture once more to point a nation toward its Maker: "As we've been assured, neither death nor life nor angels nor principalities, nor powers nor things present nor things to come nor height nor depth," he said, quoting Romans 8:38–39, "can separate us from God's love."[6]

Notes

1. Howard Fineman, "Bush and God," *Newsweek*, 10 Mar 2003.
2. John C. McCollister, *God and the Oval Office* (Nashville: W Publishing Group, 2005), 235.
3. Mike Evans, *The Final Move Beyond Iraq* (Lake Mary, FL: FrontLine, 2007), 38.
4. Craig Etheredge, "George W. Bush," *Morning Thrive*, 27 Jan 2017, http://firstcolleyville.com /blogs/morning-thrive-george-w-bush.
5. McCollister, *God and the Oval Office*, 236.
6. George W. Bush, "Remarks at the National Day of Prayer & Remembrance Service," *American Rhetoric*, 14 Sep 2001, http://www.americanrhetoric.com/speeches/gwbush911 prayer&memorialaddress.htm.

11

ANDRÉ CARSON

US Representative from Indiana

Education and Equality

The father, if he educates his daughter well, will enter paradise.

—*Hadith of the Prophet Muhammad*

O people! Indeed, your Lord is one and your father is one. Indeed, there is no superiority of an Arab over a non-Arab, nor of a non-Arab over an Arab, nor of a white over a black, nor a black over a white.

—*Muhammad's final sermon*
(Reported in Musnad Ahmad ibn Hanbal*)*

Winning a special election in 2008 to succeed his late grandmother, Rep. Julia Carson, André Carson became the second Muslim to serve in the US Congress. He grew up attending a Baptist church and a Catholic school, but he was converted to Islam when he was sixteen or seventeen. He was impressed with *The Autobiography of Malcolm X,* the poetry of the Sufi mystic Rumi, and the way Muslims in the community were "pushing back on crime and protecting the neighborhood," he said.[1]

The young Carson was also drawn to the Qur'an, finding that the teachings in that book brought answers to the theological questions that had been "stirring his intellectual curiosity." He was so impressed with the Qur'an that later as a congressman he held it up as a standard that was helping some Muslim schools succeed in the inner city over some public schools.

"America will never tap into educational innovation and ingenuity without looking at the model that we have in our madrassas, in our schools," he said, "where innovation is encouraged, where the foundation is the Quran."[2]

The comment, especially when taken out of context, caused some controversy. "While I do not believe that any particular faith should be the foundation of our public schools," Carson quickly clarified, "it is important that we take note of the instructional tools these schools utilize to empower their young people. Christian, Jewish, and Islamic schools have experienced notable success by casting off a one-size-fits-all approach to education, and this is a model we must replicate."[3]

Carson once commented on the fact that he didn't find it surprising that the first Muslim members of Congress were from Minnesota and Indiana. "I'm in the Bible Belt, but what you'll find about Midwesterners is that they're less concerned about what religion a person is and more concerned with their value system and whether they'll deliver," he said.

"What you are seeing from Representative Ellison and myself are Muslims that come from the African-American experience. We are more concerned with civil and human rights, with education, with the global economy, creating jobs and how to repair broken infrastructure. These are issues Midwesterners relate to."

Carson, a Democrat, has also shared his favorite scriptures, which regard education and equality. "It was the Prophet Mohammed, peace be upon him, who stated explicitly in the Hadith that a man who educates his daughters is granted paradise. I think that has figurative implications and political implications," he said. "In the prophet's last sermon he said there is no superiority—white over black, Arab over non-Arab—words that were quite visionary and also applicable to our times today."[4]

NOTES

1. Paul Vale, "Muslim Congressman Andre Carson On The Bible Belt, Equal Marriage, Madrassas And An LGBT President," *HuffPost United Kingdom,* 21 Nov 2014, http://www .huffingtonpost.co.uk/2014/11/20/muslim-congressman-andre-carson-_n_6189790.html.

See also, "Andre Carson," *Discover the Networks*, last updated 26, Oct 2018, http://www.discoverthenetworks.org/individualProfile.asp?indid=2552.

2. Caroline May, "Rep. Carson: America's schools should use madrassas as 'model,' 'where the foundation is the Koran,'" *The Daily Caller*, 5 Jul 2012, http://dailycaller.com/2012/07/05/rep-carson-americas-schools-should-use-madrassas-as-model.

3. Laura Hibbard, "André Carson, Indiana Congressman, Says U.S. Public Schools Should Be Modeled After Islamic Schools," *Huffington Post*, 6 Jul 2012, http://www.huffingtonpost.com/2012/07/06/andre-carson-schools-should-be-modeled-after-madrassa_n_1654510.html.

4. Vale, "Muslim Congressman."

12

BEN CARSON

US Secretary of Housing and Urban Affairs

Success from God

By humility and the fear of the Lord are riches, and honour, and life.

—Proverbs 22:4 (KJV)

The former presidential candidate and famed neurosurgeon is also a lifelong Seventh-day Adventist with a love for the Bible. Ben Carson was actually baptized twice, first at Detroit's Burns Seventh-day Adventist Church, and then again at age twelve when he told the pastor at the suburban Inkster Seventh-day Adventist Church that he didn't fully understand his first baptism and wanted to do it again.

As an adult, Carson has been a Sabbath School teacher and an Adventist local elder, but he also enjoys attending other Christian denominations. "I spend just as much time in non-Seventh-day Adventist churches because I'm not convinced that the denomination is the most important thing," he said. "I think it's the relationship with God that's most important."[1]

When asked on the campaign trail what sets him apart from one of his opponents, he said, "I've realized where my success has come from, and I don't in any way deny my faith in God." He then quoted Proverbs 22:4: "'By humility and the fear of the Lord are riches, and honour, and life,'" he said, "and that's a very big part of who I am."[2]

In an interview with Megyn Kelly on Fox News, Carson shared that some of his favorite verses of scripture are Proverbs 22:4 (quoted above) and Proverbs 3:5–6. "Trust in the Lord with all thine heart; and lean not unto thine own understanding," it reads. "In all thy ways acknowledge him, and he shall direct thy paths." Carson said, "I realize where my successes come from, and I don't in any way deny my faith in God."[3]

NOTES

1. Adelle M. Banks and Cathy Lynn Grossman, "5 faith facts about Ben Carson: Retired neurosurgeon, Seventh-day Adventist," *Religion News Service,* 1 Feb 2016, http://religionnews.com/2016/02/01/ben-carson-religion-adventist-evangelical/.
2. Barton Swaim, "The pitfalls of politicians citing Bible verses," *Washington Post,* 2 Dec 2015, https://www.washingtonpost.com/news/the-fix/wp/2015/12/02/if-a-2016-candidate-is-citing-a-bible-verse-theres-a-good-chance-its-not-quite-right.
3. Ray Nothstine, "Ben Carson, Unlike Donald Trump, Can Name His Favorite Bible Verses," *Christian Post,* 10 Sep 2015, http://www.christianpost.com/news/ben-carson-unlike-donald-trump-can-name-his-favorite-bible-verses-144923/.

13

JIMMY CARTER

Thirty-Ninth President of the United States

Things Not Seen

So we fix our eyes not on what is seen, but on what is unseen, since what is seen is temporary, but what is unseen is eternal.

—*2 Corinthians 4:18 (NIV)*

Jimmy Carter loves the Bible and is probably more familiar with its pages than any modern president. "I've been teaching Bible lessons since I was eighteen years old," he said. "I was a midshipman at Annapolis and I taught Sunday School every Sunday. I taught Bible lessons on the submarine, I taught Bible lessons when I was a farmer, I taught Sunday School at the First Baptist Church in Washington about fifteen times while I was actually president, and since then I've been teaching at my local church in Plains [Georgia]."[1]

When he was sworn in as president, Carter used a family Bible and George Washington's Bible, which were opened to Micah 6:8, also one of Washington's favorites. "I have just taken the oath of office on the Bible my mother gave me a few years ago," he said in his inaugural address, "opened to a timeless admonition from the ancient prophet Micah."[2]

Later, when asked what his favorite verses were, he said, "Everybody likes John 3:16, and everybody likes the statement of Paul's that we are saved through the grace of God, through our faith in Jesus Christ, and the first verse of the eighth chapter of Romans. [Therefore, there is now no condemnation for those who are in Christ Jesus.] . . . These are a few of my favorites."

Yet in that exchange, Jimmy Carter spent the bulk of his answer explaining one particular verse that is especially significant to him:

> There is a strange passage in Second Corinthians that I use every now and then [quoted above], where the Corinthians came to Paul and said, "What is important? What is permanent?" And Paul said, "The things you cannot see." And they were quizzical about what that meant. And he said the things that people desire and are their main ambitions for money, and a beautiful life, public approbation, fame, and security, and even life are the things we spend our existence working to achieve. It's legitimate ambitions, but Paul said those are insignificant in the eyes of God.
>
> What is significant are the things you cannot see, and of course the things you cannot see are the principles of Jesus Christ. He had no money, he did not have any ostentatious house, he didn't even have a donkey to ride on, apparently. He was abandoned by his friends, his fame dissipated at the time of his trial and execution. He only lived to be thirty-three years old, but he exemplifies all the things that are important in the eyes of God. And that is a kind of provocative part of the Bible that I like to think about often.[3]

NOTES

1. "Teaching the Bible with President Jimmy Carter," *Beliefnet*, retrieved 4 Apr 2017, http:// www.beliefnet.com/faiths/christianity/articles/teaching-the-bible-with-jimmy-carter.aspx#Km 0gAyfpCFKLMGBs.99.
2. "The 48th Presidential Inauguration," Joint Congressional Committee on Inaugural Ceremonies, retrieved 11 Apr 2017, https://www.inaugural.senate.gov/about/past -inaugural-ceremonies/48th-inaugural-ceremonies.
3. "President Carter: His Favorite Bible Passage," *Beliefnet*, retrieved 30 Apr 2017, http://www .beliefnet.com/video/news-and-politics/jimmy-carter/president-carter-his-favorite-bible -passage.aspx.

14

CHRIS CHRISTIE

Governor of New Jersey

Go Out with Joy

You will go out in joy and be led forth in peace; the mountains and hills will burst into song before you, and all the trees of the field will clap their hands.

—Isaiah 55:12 (NIV)

C hris Christie was raised in a Roman Catholic family and considers being Catholic "a huge part" of his identity. He often tells the story of going to Mass with his grandmother as a boy and learning to pray. When he prayed before a test and only got a C, he complained that praying doesn't work. His grandma told him, "God always answers your prayers; sometimes the answer is 'no.'"

Christie's wife, Mary Pat, was the ninth of ten children in a devout Irish-Catholic family. The couple attends St. Joseph's Church, a Catholic parish in Mendham, New Jersey, when they are able. The Christies have also sent their four children to parochial schools. Catholic school reinforces "the tenet of our faith that says we must treat our brother as we would like to be treated ourselves," Christie said.[1]

While running for the Republican nomination for president, Christie didn't wear his religion on his sleeve like many of his competitors, but he did show his faith at times. In his Christmas card to Iowa Republicans, Christie had next to his family picture the verse from Isaiah that says, "You will go out in joy and be led forth in peace" (quoted above). He really liked the verse, and he used it again the next Christmas, too.[2]

NOTES

1. Kelly Heyboer, "Chris Christie's religion: 7 facts about his Catholic faith," *NJ.com,* 2 Aug 2015, http://www.nj.com/politics/index.ssf/2015/08/chris_christies_religion_7_facts_about_his_catholi.html.
2. Chase Brush, "Iowa Republicans Get a Chris Christie Christmas Card," *Observer,* 24 Dec 2014, http://observer.com/2014/12/iowa-republicans-get-a-chris-christie-christmas-card.

15

GROVER CLEVELAND

Twenty-Second and Twenty-Fourth
President of the United States

Lord Delivering, Answering, Honoring

They shall bear thee up in their hands, lest thou dash thy foot against a stone.

Thou shalt tread upon the lion and adder: the young lion and the dragon shalt thou trample under feet.

Because he hath set his love upon me, therefore will I deliver him: I will set him on high, because he hath known my name.

He shall call upon me, and I will answer him: I will be with him in trouble; I will deliver him, and honour him.

With long life will I satisfy him, and shew him my salvation.

—Psalm 91:12–16 (KJV)

Cleveland was the son of devout Presbyterian parents, and learning the stories of the Bible was an important part of his upbringing. "I have always felt that my training as a minister's son has been more valuable to me as a strengthening influence than any other incident in my life," he said in 1853.[1]

When he was sworn in as president in 1885 (the first Democrat since before the Civil War), he placed his left hand on a Bible that had been given to him by his mother when he was fifteen years old. The Bible was opened by Chief Justice Morrison Waite and happened to fall open to Psalm 112:4–10.[2] Cleveland went on to complete his first term as president, but he lost reelection to Benjamin Harrison, even though Cleveland won the popular vote.

When Cleveland made his comeback four years later, he denied Harrison *his* reelection and became the only American president to serve two non-consecutive terms. Determined to do his second term better, he was off to an auspicious start when he was sworn in on the same Bible he had treasured since childhood. This time, however, he wasn't going to merely have the book open at random, but he specifically had it opened to Psalm 91:12–16 (quoted above).[3]

"I know there is a Supreme Being who rules in the affairs of men and whose goodness and mercy have always followed the American people," Cleveland said moments later in his second inaugural address, "and I know He will not turn from us now if we humbly and reverently seek His powerful aid."[4]

NOTES

1. *New York Observer*, vol. 90, 22 Jun 1911, p. 790.
2. "The 25th Presidential Inauguration," Joint Congressional Committee on Inaugural Ceremonies, retrieved 11 Apr 2017 https://www.inaugural.senate.gov/about/past-inaugural-ceremonies/25th-inaugural-ceremonies/.
3. "The 27th Presidential Inauguration," Joint Congressional Committee on Inaugural Ceremonies, retrieved 11 Apr 2017 https://www.inaugural.senate.gov/about/past-inaugural-ceremonies/27th-inaugural-ceremonies/.
4. "Second Inaugural Address of Grover Cleveland," 4 Mar 1893, *The Avalon Project*, http://avalon.law.yale.edu/19th_century/cleve2.asp.

16

BILL CLINTON

Forty-Second President of the United States

Not Weary in Well Doing

Bear ye one another's burdens, and so fulfil the law of Christ.

For if a man think himself to be something, when he is nothing, he deceiveth himself.

But let every man prove his own work, and then shall he have rejoicing in himself alone, and not in another.

For every man shall bear his own burden.

Let him that is taught in the word communicate unto him that teacheth in all good things.

Be not deceived; God is not mocked: for whatsoever a man soweth, that shall he also reap.

For he that soweth to his flesh shall of the flesh reap corruption; but he that soweth to the Spirit shall of the Spirit reap life everlasting.

And let us not be weary in well doing: for in due season we shall reap, if we faint not.

—Galatians 6:2–9 (KJV)

B ill Clinton, the baby boomer Baptist from Hope, Arkansas, was not afraid to quote scripture. "Where there is no vision, the people perish," he said in his acceptance of the Democratic nomination for president in 1992 (Proverbs 29:18).[1]

"And they that shall be of thee shall build the old waste places: thou shalt raise up the foundations of many generations," said the words of Isaiah 58:12 that Clinton placed his inaugural hand on in 1997, "and thou shalt be called, The repairer of the breach, The restorer of paths to dwell in."[2]

But it is Galatians 6 that is this Democrat's favorite, especially verse nine (quoted above). Author John Gartner said, "His philosophy was summarized in his favorite scripture, one that [advisor Paul] Begala said he quoted more often than any other, Galatians 6:9: 'Let us not become weary in doing good.'"

"Clinton used this passage in his 1990 gubernatorial inauguration, and then again in his first presidential inauguration. In this passage, we see a perfect confluence of Clinton's biology and ideology," said Gartner. "It was a passage he quoted to inspire himself, pump himself up, and keep himself going full bore, as he believed Galatians commanded him."[3]

Clinton quoted Galatians 6 more than any other scripture. In 1993, he invoked verse nine in a tribute to the late Martin Luther King Jr. Later that year, in celebrating World Youth Day in Denver with Pope John Paul II, he shared the verse again.

"At the end of our meeting the Holy Father presented me with a Bible," he said. "And so, I close with a verse from it that I think characterizes his work that we are doing here, the exhortation in St. Paul's letter to the Galatians." In 1994, Clinton shared Galatians 6:9 as part of his remarks at the Brandenburg Gate in Berlin.

At the National Prayer Breakfast in 1996, Clinton quoted Galatians 6 again, this time verses two and five: "Galatians says, 'Let everyone bear his own burden,' and then just a couple of verses later says, 'Bear one another's burden,'" he said. "Would God, through Saint Paul, have given us such contradictory advice? No, I don't think so. I think being personally responsible and reaching out to others are the two sides of humanity's coin. And we cannot live full lives, we cannot be enlarged, unless we do both."

Bill Clinton loved Galatians 6 and quoted verses from it again while honoring Ruth and Billy Graham in 1996, in part of his eulogy for Commerce Secretary Ron Brown in 1996, at the Congressional Black Caucus Foundation dinner in 2000, in his remarks on World AIDS Day in 2000, and more.[4]

"And so, my fellow Americans, as we stand at the edge of the twenty-first century, let us begin anew with energy and hope, with faith and discipline," Clinton said in his first inaugural address, moments after placing his hand on a Bible opened to Galatians 6:8. "And let us work until our work is done. The Scripture says, 'And let us not be weary in well doing: for in due season we shall reap, if we faint not.' [Galatians 6:9] From this joyful mountaintop of celebration we hear a call to service in the valley. We have heard the trumpets. We have changed the guard. And now, each in our own way and with God's help, we must answer the call."[5]

NOTES

1. Barton Swaim, "The pitfalls of politicians citing Bible verses," *Washington Post*, 2 Dec 2015, https://www.washingtonpost.com/news/the-fix/wp/2015/12/02/if-a-2016-candidate-is-citing-a-bible-verse-theres-a-good-chance-its-not-quite-right.
2. "The 53rd Presidential Inauguration," Joint Congressional Committee on Inaugural Ceremonies, retrieved 11 Apr 2017, https://www.inaugural.senate.gov/about/past-inaugural-ceremonies/53rd-inaugural-ceremonies.
3. John Gartner, *In Search of Bill Clinton: A Psychological Biography* (New York: St. Martin's Press, 2008), 152.
4. Documents archived by the Clinton Presidential Library, retrieved 8 May 2017, https://clinton.presidentiallibraries.us.
5. "The 52nd Presidential Inauguration," Joint Congressional Committee on Inaugural Ceremonies, retrieved 11 Apr 2017, https://www.inaugural.senate.gov/about/past-inaugural-ceremonies/52nd-inaugural-ceremonies.

17

HILLARY CLINTON

US Secretary of State

Acting Out of Love

Do to others as you would have them do to you.

—*Luke 6:31 (New Revised Standard Version of the Bible)*

Whether as the Democratic nominee for president, Secretary of State, US Senator, or First Lady, Hillary Rodham Clinton spent decades in the public eye. Through the rough and tumble of a political life, Clinton has drawn strength from the words of holy scripture.

"The Bible was and remains the biggest influence on my thinking," she once told the *New York Times*. "I was raised reading it, memorizing passages from it, and being guided by it. . . . I still find it a source of wisdom, comfort, and encouragement."[1] She once told a Baptist minister she met in South Carolina, "I have a preacher friend who sends me scripture and devotionals, sometimes mini-sermons, every day." Of the Bible, she said, "It's the living word."[2]

She developed a love of the Bible as a young girl attending First Methodist Church in Park Ridge, Illinois. "I loved that church; I loved how it made me feel about myself; I loved the doors that it opened in my understanding of the world," she said.[3] Both her parents came from a long line of Methodist families, "and they claimed," Clinton said of her ancestors, "going back many years, to have actually been converted by John and Charles Wesley. And, of course, Methodists—we are methodical. It was a particularly good religion for me."[4]

Her Methodist upbringing shaped her religious worldview, providing an outlook where doing good is coupled with faith. Once, while speaking at the Saddleback Church in Lake Forest, California, she shared that one of her favorite passages was "the line from James: 'Faith without works is dead.'" She used it to compliment the megachurch. "Here, in what you're doing, faith and works come together—and you understand that," she said. "And what extraordinary, important work your faith supports."[5]

On another occasion, Clinton explained how this perspective drives her to make a difference. "We can't do it just by wishing for it. We can't do it just by hoping for it," she said. "Prayer helps, but hard work also is something we gotta do together. You know, I'm a Methodist, and we believe in doing all the good that you can every day that you can. And that means we come together and we set some goals and we go about achieving them."[6]

Once, at a White House Prayer Breakfast, Hillary Clinton elaborated on her Methodist way of living out her faith. "We believe that faith without works may not be dead, but it is hard to discern from time to time. John Wesley had this simple rule which I carry around with me as I travel: 'Do all the good you can by all the means you can and by all the ways you can and all the places you can at all times you can to all the people you can, as long as you ever can.' . . . It was a good rule to be raised by, and it was certainly a good rule for my mother and father to discipline us by. And I think it is a good rule to live by, with the appropriate dose of humility."[7]

Complimenting this appreciation of doctrines of action, Clinton also values the Golden Rule and Sermon on the Mount, taught in the New Testament. "One cannot read the Sermon on the Mount without thinking that we all have to be more humble," she said in an interview with ABC News. "We all have to be more kind and respectful."[8]

In a Democratic debate in New Hampshire, the candidates were asked to share their favorite Bible verses. "The Golden Rule: Do unto others as you would have them do unto you," Clinton replied unflinchingly. "I think that's a good rule for politics, too."[9]

She has talked about the universal application of the Golden Rule. "The teachings of every religion call us to care for the poor, tell us to visit the orphans and widows, to be generous and charitable, to alleviate suffering," Clinton said. "All religions have their version of the Golden Rule and direct us to love our neighbor and welcome the stranger and visit the prisoner. But how often in our own lives do we respond to that? All of these holy texts, all of this religious wisdom from these very different faiths, call on us to act out of love."[10]

NOTES

1. Barton Swaim, "The pitfalls of politicians citing Bible verses," *Washington Post,* 2 Dec 2015, https://www.washingtonpost.com/news/the-fix/wp/2015/12/02/if-a-2016-candidate-is-citing-a-bible-verse-theres-a-good-chance-its-not-quite-right.

2. Dan Merica, "With scripture, Hillary Clinton wins over a voter," *CNN,* 28 May 2015, http://www.cnn.com/2015/05/27/politics/hillary-clinton-2016-election-faith/.

3. Ibid.

4. Hillary Clinton, "Remarks at White House Prayer Breakfast," *Congressional Record—Senate, Vol. 156, Pt. 8, p. 10807,* 16 Jun 2010.

5. Carla Marinucci, "Clinton, Democrats find religion, court evangelical voters," *San Francisco Chronicle,* 30 Nov 2007, http://www.sfgate.com/politics/article/Clinton-Democrats-find-religion-court-3300251.php.

6. Hillary Rodham Clinton, "Hillary Clinton on the Methodist Goal of Daily Doing Good," *Berkeley Center for Religion, Peace & World Affairs,* 5 May 2008, https://berkleycenter.georgetown.edu/quotes/hillary-clinton-on-the-methodist-goal-of-daily-doing-good.

7. Clinton, "Remarks at White House Prayer Breakfast."

8. Swaim, "The pitfalls of politicians citing Bible verses."

9. Jeff Zeleny, "The Democrats Quote Scripture," *New York Times,* 27 Sep 2007, https://thecaucus.blogs.nytimes.com/2007/09/27/the-democrats-quote-scripture/.

10. Clinton, "Remarks at White House Prayer Breakfast."

18

JIM CLYBURN

US Representative from South Carolina

Giving Credence to Faith

Now faith is the substance of things hoped for, the evidence of things not seen.

—Hebrews 11:1 (KJV)

Jim Clyburn has represented his home state of South Carolina in Congress since 1993, but long before that he grew up in a home where he became well acquainted with what he calls "the greatest of all books, the Bible."

"When I was growing up, my father, who was a fundamentalist minister, never asked me to read the Bible, never instructed me to do so," Clyburn explains. "He just told me every morning at the breakfast table to recite a Bible verse. Now, it would be a little difficult to do that without reading the Bible. He made sure that we didn't do the same one twice. Daddy set down the rule. He took Jesus's whip off the table. So it was very, very important for me to read the Bible daily."

Clyburn, one of the Democratic leaders in the House, explained to his colleagues that his favorite book in the Bible is James in the New Testament.

"It's a very short book, but it tells us a lot about our responsibility. There, in the second chapter of James, we are all instructed that if your brother or sister comes to you hungry and naked, it is not enough to tell them to go in faith; you feed them and you clothe them." (See James 2:15–16.)

Clyburn continued, applying James to his work in the House of Representatives. "That is what this Congress is all about. This Congress is about doing those things that are necessary to make sure that our constituents and make sure that our citizens are fed that need to be fed or clothed that need to be clothed," he said. "I do believe if James were writing his epistle today, he would also tell us it is also important to house them when they need shelter."

A specific verse in scripture that Clyburn has highlighted publicly is Hebrews 11:1 (quoted above). "I call that the faith chapter of the Bible," he said. "In our work here, much of the time, though we don't view our work as being grounded in the Bible, we often strike out on faith." He continued, "We have a little idea sometimes of exactly where any issue is going. I do believe that as we carry out our duties and responsibilities to the people of this great Nation, sometimes we ought to pause and give credence to where that emanates from."[1]

NOTE

1. Congressional Record, 110th Congress, 1st Session, Issue: Vol. 153, No. 170, 5 Nov 2007, https://www.congress.gov/congressional-record/2007/11/05/house-section/article/H12486-2.

19

CALVIN COOLIDGE

Thirtieth President of the United States

God Is the Light of Men

In the beginning was the Word, and the Word was with God, and the Word was God.

The same was in the beginning with God.

All things were made by him; and without him was not any thing made that was made.

In him was life; and the life was the light of men.

—John 1:1–4 (KJV)

An unassumingly quiet, strictly moral, and rigidly honest New England Puritan, John Calvin Coolidge believed in America's righteous might. "The legions which she sends forth are armed, not with the sword, but with the cross," he said in his 1925 inaugural address.[1]

When administered the oath of office by Chief Justice and former president William Howard Taft, Coolidge had open a family Bible, given to him by his mother, to John 1. It is unknown why the chapter stood out to

Coolidge, but it is notable as the only passage ever selected for an inauguration that is explicitly Christological.

"The strength of our country is the strength of its religious convictions," the Republican president wrote in 1923. "The foundations of our society and our government rest so much on the teachings of the Bible that it would be difficult to support them if faith in these teachings would cease to be practically universal in our country."[2]

NOTES

1. "The 35th Presidential Inauguration," Joint Congressional Committee on Inaugural Ceremonies, retrieved 11 Apr 2017, https://www.inaugural.senate.gov/about/past-inaugural -ceremonies/35th-inaugural-ceremonies/.
2. William J. Federer, *America's God and Country: Encyclopedia of Quotations* (St. Louis: Amerisearch, 2000), 181.

20

TED CRUZ

US Senator from Texas

Morning Is Coming

For his anger endureth but a moment; in his favour is life: weeping may endure for a night, but joy cometh in the morning.

—*Psalm 30:5 (KJV)*

Ted Cruz was born in Calgary to a mother from Delaware and a Cuban father, who later became a preacher, and jokes, "I'm Cuban, Irish, and Italian, and yet somehow I ended up Southern Baptist."[1] Ted Cruz is the first Hispanic senator from Texas and was one of the leading candidates for the Republican nomination in 2016.

In the words of Messiah College professor John Fea, "There have been few presidential candidates in United States history with such bona fide God-and-country credentials." He points out that "Ted Cruz was raised in an evangelical subculture. He grew up studying the Bible and was taught to integrate faith and learning at Second Baptist School in Houston."

His biblical faith permeates his campaign rhetoric and his Senate speeches. For example, while stumping at Community Bible Church in

Beaufort, South Carolina, he reminded the congregants the words of Psalm 30:5, "Weeping may endure for a night, but joy comes in the morning," and promises them that "morning is coming."[2]

Cruz is inspired by that verse and often inspires audiences with it. He also shared it during his victory speech following the 2016 Iowa caucuses. "Our rights do not come from the Democratic Party or the Republican Party or even from the Tea Party. Our rights come from our Creator," he said to cheers in Des Moines.

"The federal government's responsibility is to defend those rights, defend us. And while Americans will continue to suffer under a president who has set an agenda that is causing millions to hurt across this country, I want to remind you of the promise of Scripture—'Weeping may endure for a night but joy cometh in the morning,'" said Cruz. "Tonight Iowa has proclaimed to the world, 'Morning is coming, morning is coming.'"[3]

NOTES

1. "Texan of the Year finalist Ted Cruz," *Dallas Morning News*, Dec 2012, https://www.dallasnews.com/opinion/editorials/2012/12/20/editorial-texan-of-the-year-finalist-ted-cruz.
2. John Fea, "The Theology of Ted Cruz," *Christianity Today*, 1 Apr 2016, http://www.christianitytoday.com/ct/2016/april-web-only/religion-of-ted-cruz.html?start=1.
3. Leonardo Blair, "Ted Cruz Quotes Scripture, Thanks God and 'Courageous Conservatives' after Iowa Victory," *Christian Post*, 2 Feb 2016, http://www.christianpost.com/news/ted-cruz-quotes-scripture-thanks-god-iowa-caucus-156562/.

21

ANDREW CUOMO

Governor of New York

Reap What Is Sown

For they have sown the wind, and they shall reap the whirlwind: it hath no stalk: the bud shall yield no meal: if so be it yield, the strangers shall swallow it up.

—Hosea 8:7 (KJV)

The governor of New York comes from a Catholic family of immigrants. "I am a son of immigrants," he said. "Son of Mario Cuomo, who is the son of Andrea Cuomo, a poor, Italian immigrant who came to this country without a job, without money or resources, and he was here only for the promise of America."

Cuomo grew up with priests and bishops as guests for dinner at their home and attended Catholic schools, like Archbishop Molloy High School and Fordham University. He does not consider himself a devout Roman Catholic, but he does consider himself a practicing Catholic—occasionally attending Mass, agreeing with the pope on opposing the death penalty, but differing on same-sex marriage and abortion.[1]

In a strongly worded speech responding to the hateful rhetoric sweeping the nation after the 2016 elections, the Democratic governor shared scripture: "There are many who are soul sick for their America. There are young and old who feel alienated, disrespected, and confused by what they hear," he said. "We can now begin to understand what the Old Testament meant when it said they that sow the wind shall reap the whirlwind [Hosea 8:7]. We are in a whirlwind of hate and division all across this country."

He went on to say that the answer is in the Golden Rule, which he said "is the bedrock for faith for people around the world." Then the governor quoted Matthew and Leviticus, saying, "Love thy neighbor as thyself." Cuomo went on,

> This belief in loving thy neighbor, the Golden Rule, is repeated throughout the Koran by the prophet Muhammad, who said, "None of you has faith until he loves for his brother what he loves for himself."
>
> Long before the East and West met, Confucius wrote in 500 B.C., "Never impose on others what you would not choose for yourself."
>
> Even the Sanskrit traditions of ancient India taught us, "Treat others as you would treat yourself."
>
> It is a timeless truth and these are the words that we need to take to heart at these dark times.[2]

NOTES

1. Paul Vitello, "A Cuomo Who Is Catholic but Hardly Theological," *New York Times*, 18 Mar 2011, http://www.nytimes.com/2011/03/19/nyregion/19cuomo.html.
2. Jen Chung, "Cuomo Gives Inspiring Speech: 'NY Still Knows What America Is Supposed to Be,'" *Gothamist*, 20 Nov 2016, http://gothamist.com/2016/11/20/cuomo_inspiring_speech_against_hate.php.

22

DWIGHT D. EISENHOWER

Thirty-Fourth President of the United States

A Nation under God

If my people, which are called by my name, shall humble themselves, and pray, and seek my face, and turn from their wicked ways; then will I hear from heaven, and will forgive their sin, and will heal their land.

—*2 Chronicles 7:14 (KJV)*

Blessed is the nation whose God is the Lord; and the people whom he hath chosen for his own inheritance.

—*Psalm 33:12 (KJV)*

Dwight David Eisenhower, the hero of World War II, was a God-fearing man who had learned to revere the Holy Scriptures in his youth. "I am the most intensely religious man I know," the general-turned-president once said. "Nobody goes through six years of war without faith."[1]

When he was being sworn in as president, he placed his left hand on top of two Bibles. One was Washington's Bible, which he had opened to

2 Chronicles 7:14. The other was his personal Bible he had used since he was a cadet at West Point, which he had turned to Psalm 33:12.[2]

The verse in Chronicles was part of the Lord's acceptance of Solomon's temple and has been a popular verse used by several presidents. Psalm 33 was unique to Eisenhower and so beloved by him that when he was sworn in for his second term in 1957, he used just one Bible that time (his West Point one) and just one verse—Psalm 33:12 once again.

Both verses share the theme of a nation choosing to have God as their Lord, calling on His name, and turning from wicked ways. Eisenhower sought to lead the nation back from the trend of secularization and toward the God of Heaven. He was the first to begin his inaugural address with a prayer, he was the first president to be baptized while in office (at the National Presbyterian Church less than two weeks after his inaugural), and in 1954 the Republican president added the phrase "under God" to the Pledge of Allegiance.

He did his best to act on his beloved Psalm 33:12, encouraging the nation to remember their God. When he signed the bill into law adding God into the Pledge of Allegiance, he declared, "From this day forward, the millions of our school children will daily proclaim in every city and town, every village and rural school house, the dedication of our nation and our people to the Almighty."[3]

NOTES

1. "God in the White House," *PBS*, retrieved 4 Apr 2017, http://www.pbs.org/godinamerica /god-in-the-white-house.
2. "The 43rd Presidential Inauguration," Joint Congressional Committee on Inaugural Ceremonies, retrieved 11 Apr 2017, https://www.inaugural.senate.gov/about/past-inaugural -ceremonies/43rd-inaugural-ceremonies.
3. "Statement by the President upon Signing Bill to Include the Words 'Under God' in the Pledge to the Flag," 14 Jun 1954, in Gerhard Peters and John T. Woolley, *The American Presidency Project*, retrieved 16 Apr 2017, http://www.presidency.ucsb.edu/ws/?pid=9920.

23

KEITH ELLISON

US Representative from Minnesota

Family of Humanity

Oh, humanity, we created you from a single pair, male and female, and made you tribes and nations so that you would know each other and not despise each other. Verily the most honoured of you in the sight of Allah is he who is the most righteous of you. And Allah has full knowledge and is well acquainted with all things.

—Al-Hujurat 49:13 (Yusuf Ali translation of the Qur'an)

Minnesota's Keith Ellison, the first Muslim ever elected to the United States Congress, grew up in a Catholic home in Detroit, Michigan. "I can't claim that I was the most observant Catholic at the time," he said of himself at age nineteen while attending Wayne State University. "I had begun to really look around and ask myself about the social circumstances of the country, issues of justice, issues of change. When I looked at my spiritual life, and I looked at what might inform social change, justice in society . . . I found Islam."[1]

When elected to Congress in November 2006 to represent Minnesota's fifth congressional district, an anonymous person told Ellison that Thomas Jefferson had a personal copy of the Qur'an located in the Library of Congress and suggested that he use it to be sworn in on. He liked the idea, but controversy erupted when it was announced. Conservative media pundit Dennis Prager, Rep. Virgil Goode of Virginia, and others expressed their discomfort with a member of Congress not being sworn in on the traditional Bible.

Despite the uproar, Ellison was indeed sworn in on Jefferson's Qur'an, a two-volume version of the scripture the third president had purchased in 1765 while studying for the bar exam to become a lawyer. The book was a 1734 edition of the first Arabic to English translation, and it was lent by the Library of Congress for the occasion.[2]

"It demonstrates that from the very beginning of our country, we had people who were visionary, who were religiously tolerant, who believed that knowledge and wisdom could be gleaned from any number of sources, including the Quran," Ellison told the Associated Press about the symbolism of the act.

"A visionary like Thomas Jefferson was not afraid of a different belief system," the Democratic congressman said. "This just shows that religious tolerance is the bedrock of our country, and religious differences are nothing to be afraid of."[3]

To demonstrate his view that all of humanity is one family, and perhaps to help calm down those uncomfortable with a Muslim in Congress, Ellison shared an inclusive verse from the Qur'an at a multi-faith prayer service the morning he was sworn in. "Oh, humanity, we created you from a single pair, male and female," said part of the verse found in Al-Hujurat 49:13, "and made you into tribes and nations, so that you would know each other and not despise each other."[4]

NOTES

1. Todd Melby, "Keith Ellison May Be the First Muslim in U.S. Congress," *Boston Globe*, 17 Sep 2006.
2. "Thomas Jefferson's Copy of the Koran to Be Used in Congressional Swearing-in Ceremony," *Library of Congress*, 3 Jan 2007, https://www.loc.gov/item/prn-07-001/.
3. Frederic J. Frommer, "Congressman Uses Thomas Jefferson's Quran at swearing in," *Seattle Times*, 4 Jan 2007, http://old.seattletimes.com/html/faithvalues/2003509142_webellison04.html.
4. Sean Mussenden, "110th Congress: Goode Offers Greetings to Muslim Lawmaker," *Richmond-Times Dispatch*, Jan. 5, 2007, archived copy retrieved Jun. 4, 2017, https://web.archive.org/web/20070927131155/http://george.loper.org/~george/archives/2007/Jan/984.html.

24

MARY FALLIN

Governor of Oklahoma

We All Need God

For where two or three are gathered together in My name, I am there among them.

—Matthew 18:20 (Holman Christian Standard Bible)

A past legislator, lieutenant governor, member of Congress, and chair of the National Governors Association, Mary Fallin is the governor of Oklahoma and a believer in God and the Bible.

"The most important thing about me is I love God. And I'm a Christian. And I'm not scared to say I am," she said at a Good News Festival in Oklahoma City in 2015.

"I'm not scared to walk my faith. And my faith does play a role in the decisions that I make. I do seek God's wisdom, God's discernment, God's grace, God's forgiveness, in all the decisions that we make on behalf of the state of Oklahoma and certainly as our nation," she said.

The Republican governor proclaimed that everyone needs the help of the Almighty. "No matter who we are and what title we might hold, we all need

God. I don't know how people make it without God," she said. "But you know what? Our God is greater than evil. We know the end of the story. We know that we win."

She went on to share her view of the nation's need for God. "I want to tell you something about America. You know, America was founded on godly principles. I believe that. But America will cease to be great if America takes God out of our country."

Before concluding her remarks, Governor Fallin shared a couple of her favorite scriptures that are important to her. She shared 2 Chronicles 7:14, a verse popular with many other political leaders about the Lord healing the land of those who humble themselves before Him.

She also shared Matthew 18:20, which "says that whenever two or more are gathered together, there I am among them." She concluded, "So the good news is that God is here among us tonight. He is in this room. He knows our hearts. He knows things are going to happen to us before we even know things are going to happen. He knows the end of the story."[1]

NOTE

1. "Oklahoma Governor at Festival: 'We All Need God,'" *Billy Graham Evangelical Association*, 24 Aug 2015, https://billygraham.org/story/oklahoma-governor-at-festival-we-all-need-god.

25

JEFF FLAKE

US Senator from Arizona

Examining Ourselves

And why beholdest thou the mote that is in thy brother's eye, but considerest not the beam that is in thine own eye?

—*Matthew 7:3 (KJV)*

Jeff Flake grew up in Snowflake, Arizona—a town settled by the Latter-day Saint pioneers from the Snow and Flake families (including his ancestors). He has remained true to his heritage in The Church of Jesus Christ of Latter-day Saints and served a two-year mission as a young man to South Africa and Zimbabwe, learning to preach in Afrikaans. He graduated from the church's flagship university, Brigham Young University, with both bachelor's and master's degrees.

Partially due to the Arizona coattails of a fellow Latter-day Saint, Republican presidential nominee Mitt Romney, Flake won a close 2012 race and jumped from the House of Representatives to the Senate. When he was sworn in, he chose to use his "quad," as Latter-day Saints call their book that is a quadruple combination of the Bible, the Book of Mormon, the Doctrine and Covenants, and the Pearl of Great Price—all considered scripture by the faith.

Senator Bill Nelson, a Florida Democrat, asked to borrow Flake's Bible for his own swearing in shortly after, and Flake lent him the leather-bound combo of scriptures he was just sworn in on. Afterward, Senate Majority Leader (and fellow Latter-day Saint) Harry Reid, obviously finding humor in the situation, asked Flake when he would tell Nelson that he just took an oath on the Book of Mormon. Flake enjoyed sharing the fun anecdote at a Pioneer Day celebration in his hometown a few months later.[1]

Flake's Mormon heritage helped shape his view on President Donald Trump's ban of immigrants and refugees from several Muslim-majority nations. Relating the Missouri extermination order against the Latter-day Saints in 1838 in his latest book, Flake then pointed out that Mormons "have had foundational and horrifying experience with some of these worst impulses of mankind and became both refugees and immigrants in our own land." He continued, "So when someone starts talking of religious tests and religious bans, we know better. Because we have seen this all before. When we say 'No Muslims' or 'No Mexicans,' we may as well say 'No Mormons.' Because it is no different," the Republican senator said.[2]

In the same book, Flake invoked the New Testament to invite conservatives to examine themselves. "It will always be essential for conservatives to find energy and ideas by defining ourselves in opposition [to liberals]," he said. "But we must never shirk our obligation to examine ourselves, too. I include myself in this admonition. In that, I am reminded of the Book of Matthew: 'And why beholdest thou the mote that is in thy brother's eye, but considerest not the beam that is in thine own eye?'"[3]

NOTES

1. Naomi Hatch, "Senator Jeff Flake Returns Home to Join In Pioneer Days Celebration," *Arizona Journal,* 27 Aug 2013, http://www.azjournal.com/2013/08/07/senator-jeff-flake-returns-home-to-join-in-pioneer-days-celebration/.
2. Jeff Flake, *Conscience of a Conservative* (New York: Random House, 2017), 51.
3. Ibid., 64.

26

GERALD R. FORD

Thirty-Eighth President of the United States

Trust in the Lord

Trust in the Lord with all thine heart; and lean not unto thine own understanding.
   In all thy ways acknowledge him, and he shall direct thy paths.

—Proverbs 3:5–6 (KJV)

The final days of Nixon's presidency wore heavy on Vice President Gerald Ford and his family. With impeachment or resignation becoming more certain each day, the burden of the presidency loomed nearer. "There had never been a time in our lives when we so much needed a source of strength beyond ourselves," Betty Ford said of those days. "Jerry reminded me of the fifth and sixth verses of chapter three of the Book of Proverbs, a prayer he learned as a boy. . . . This became our prayer."[1]

When Richard Nixon did resign on August 9, 1974, the Fords grabbed the Jerusalem Bible that had been a gift to them from their son Michael, who was training to be a minister. Gerald Ford opened the book to Proverbs 3:5–6, which he said was taught to him by his mother, and which he often recited as a prayer. Betty held the book open while her husband placed his hand on it and was sworn in as president by Chief Justice Warren Burger.[2]

"In my own life and throughout my career in public service, I have found in the pages of the Bible a steady compass and a source of great strength and peace," the new Republican president told the Southern Baptist Convention. "As America enters its third century," he continued, "we could ask no better inspiration than those words of a favorite passage of mine from the Book of Proverbs: 'Trust in the Lord with all thine heart and lean not unto thine own understanding. In all thy ways acknowledge Him and He shall direct thy paths.'"[3]

NOTES

1. Les and Leslie Parrott, "A Presidential Passage from Proverbs," retrieved 30 Apr 2017, http://www.lesandleslie.com/devotions/a-presidential-passage-from-proverbs.
2. "Swearing in Bible," *Ford Presidential Library,* retrieved 30 Apr 2017, https://www.fordlibrarymuseum.gov/swearinginbible.asp.
3. Gerald R. Ford, "Remarks at the Southern Baptist Convention in Norfolk, Virginia," 15 Jun 1976, in Gerhard Peters and John T. Woolley, *The American Presidency Project*, http://www.presidency.ucsb.edu/ws/?pid=6127.

27

TULSI GABBARD

US Representative from Hawaii

Indestructible Soul

That which pervades the entire body you should know to be indestructible.
No one is able to destroy that imperishable soul.
The soul can never be cut to pieces by any weapon, nor burned by
fire, nor moistened by water, nor withered by the wind.

—Bhagavad Gita 2.17; 2.23

B orn in American Samoa to a Catholic father and a Hindu mother, Hawaiian Member of Congress Tulsi Gabbard became the first Hindu ever elected to Congress. She follows the branch of Hinduism founded by Chaitanya Mahaprabhu known as Gaudiya Vaishnavism. Vaishnava Hindus like Gabbard venerate the deity Supreme Lord Vishnu, as well as his ten primary incarnations.

"I am a practicing Hindu, a Karma Yogi," the Democratic congresswoman explained. "A core part of who I am is service and serving others. These are principles common to all faiths—of love, compassion, openness—all people are served, irrespective of background, and I will seek to continue to do that."[1]

She's proud of her upbringing in "a multiracial, multicultural, multi-faith family," saying as a result, "I believe strongly in embracing diversity." Gabbard was familiar with scripture growing up, both the New Testament and Bhagavad Gita. The Gita, a small section of the epic poem *Mahābhārata*, especially resonates with her, and she has embraced it as a spiritual guide, saying it teaches her "to maintain [her] equilibrium in either success or failure."

Taking place on the eve of a battle, the thoughts and teachings in the Bhagavad Gita involve "enlightenment, love for God, selfless service," Gabbard said, "and how each of us can succeed in our struggle on the 'battlefields' of life." Deployed with the Hawaii Army National Guard to the Middle East twice, Major Gabbard said she "found great comfort and shelter in the Bhagavad Gita's message of the eternality of the soul and God's unconditional love."[2]

When taking the oath of office as the first Hindu Member of Congress, Rep. Gabbard did so on the scripture that is sacred to her—the Bhagavad Gita. She later gave that copy of the book to Indian Prime Minister Narendra Modi when he visited the United States.[3]

She points to two of her favorite verses in the second chapter of the Bhagavad Gita, verses 17 and 23, quoted above. These verses proclaiming the indestructability of the soul were especially inspiring to Gabbard while serving in Iraq. "First thing in the morning and the last thing at night," she said, "I meditated upon the fact that my essence was spirit, not matter, that I was not my physical body, and that I didn't need to worry about death because I knew that I would continue to exist and I knew that I would be going to God."[4]

NOTES

1. Rishi Kumar, "The Indian American Contenders," *India Currents*, 10 Oct 2012, retrieved 3 Jun 2017, http://newamericamedia.org/2012/10/the-indian-american-contenders.php.

2. Stephen Prothero, "A Hindu moment for Congress," *USA Today*, 3 Jan 2013, https://www.usatoday.com/story/opinion/2013/01/03/hindu-tulsi-gabbard-congress/1808127.

3. "Narendra Modi gets Gita as gift from US lawmaker Tulsi Gabbard," *Indian Express*, retrieved 3 Jun 2017, https://indianexpress.com/photos/picture-gallery-others/modi-wows-madison-square.

4. Omar Sacirbey, "Tulsi Gabbard, Hawaii Democrat, Poised to Be Elected First Hindu in Congress," *Huffington Post*, 2 Nov 2012, http://www.huffingtonpost.com/2012/11/02/tulsi-gabbard-hawaii-democrat-hindu-in-congress_n_2062358.html.

28

JAMES A. GARFIELD

Twentieth President of the United States

Heart in the Hand of the Lord

The king's heart is in the hand of the Lord, as the rivers of water: he turneth it whithersoever he will.

—*Proverbs 21:1 (KJV)*

Known as the "Preacher President," Garfield was a lay minister for the Disciples of Christ and devout believer in the Bible. "Where the Bible is silent, there we are silent," he declared. "Where the Bible speaks, there we speak."[1]

As a minister who was known for his inspiring preaching, Garfield had learned Greek so he could read the New Testament in the original. He reluctantly left the ministry upon his election to the White House. "I resign the highest office in the land to become President of the United States," he said.[2]

When sworn in as the twentieth president in 1881, the Republican Garfield chose to have the Bible turned to Proverbs 21:1 (quoted above).[3] Surely, the devout Garfield likened himself to the king in the verse, whose "heart is in the hand of the Lord."

The river of President Garfield's path proved short, however, when he was shot just four months into office. He lingered in pain through the hot summer for three more months before passing away and returning to the God he loved.

NOTES

1. John C. McCollister, *God and the Oval Office* (Nashville: W Publishing Group, 2005), 104.
2. Forrest Wickman, "Who Was the Most Religious President of All Time?," *Slate,* 25 Sep 2012, http://www.slate.com/articles/news_and_politics/explainer/2012/09/most_religious_president _jimmy_carter_james_garfield_or_john_quincy_adams_.html.
3. "The 24th Presidential Inauguration," Joint Congressional Committee on Inaugural Ceremonies, retrieved 10 Apr 2017, https://www.inaugural.senate.gov/about/past-inaugural -ceremonies/24th-inaugural-ceremonies.

29

NEWT GINGRICH

Speaker of the US House of Representatives

Vision or Perish

Where there is no vision, the people perish: but he that keepeth the law, happy is he.

—*Proverbs 29:18 (KJV)*

The former Speaker of the House and Republican presidential candidate was raised in Pennsylvania as a Lutheran. While attending graduate school at Tulane in New Orleans, Gingrich became a Southern Baptist. In 2009, Gingrich joined the faith of his third wife, Callista—the Roman Catholic Church.

His conversion to Catholicism was a process, and he said, "Over the course of several years, I gradually became Catholic and then decided one day to accept the faith I had already come to embrace." Callista, who would later be named by President Donald Trump as United States Ambassador to the Vatican, sang in the choir of the Basilica of the National Shrine of the Immaculate Conception in Washington, DC, and Gingrich would travel with her around the world to watch her sing.

"Listening to 'Amazing Grace' being sung in Chinese at Mass in Beijing was a beautiful experience, and worshipping with believers across the world opened my eyes to the diversity and richness of the Catholic Church," Gingrich said.

In 2008, he watched Callista and her choir sing for an evening vespers service at the Basilica of the National Shrine of the Immaculate Conception. The audience included three hundred American bishops and a visiting Pope Benedict XVI. That service was the tipping point for Gingrich's conversion.

"Catching a glimpse of Pope Benedict that day, I was struck by the happiness and peacefulness he exuded," he said. "The joyful and radiating presence of the Holy Father was a moment of confirmation about the many things I had been thinking and experiencing for several years."[1]

While campaigning for the Republican presidential nomination in 2012 in Charleston, South Carolina, Gingrich spoke at the Cathedral of Praise church. He decried religious persecution around the world, including Coptic churches being burned in Egypt, and said that America must have a vision to defend religious liberties. "I believe what we need desperately in America today is captured in a simple Bible phrase: 'Without vision the people perish,'" he said, citing Proverbs 29:18.[2]

NOTES

1. Kendra Marr, "Gingrich on Why He Became a Catholic," *Politico*, 26 Apr 2011, http://www .politico.com/story/2011/04/gingrich-on-why-he-became-a-catholic-053719.
2. Alana Semuels, "Newt Gingrich Courts Churchgoers in South Carolina," *Los Angeles Times*, 15 Jan 2012, http://articles.latimes.com/2012/jan/15/news/la-pn-newt-gingrich-courts-church goers-in-south-carolina-20120115.

30

RUDY GIULIANI

Mayor of New York City

Judge Not

Do not judge, or you too will be judged. —*Matthew 7:1 (NIV)*

The former mayor of New York City who helped guide that city through the aftermath of the 9/11 attacks is the grandson of Italian immigrants and was raised in a devout Roman Catholic family. "I have very, very strong views on religion that come about from having wanted to be a priest when I was younger, having studied theology for four years in college," he said.[1]

However, "the priesthood is a vocation," Giuliani recalled, "and I probably didn't have it. I probably just thought I had it." The draw of girls and desire to give his parents grandchildren were part of it, and he said he likely would have taken holy vows "if the priesthood had encompassed marriage."[2]

As an adult, Giuliani has professed to love the Bible but doesn't take it as literally as an evangelical. "The reality is, I believe it, but I don't believe it's necessarily literally true in every single respect," he said. "I think there are parts of the Bible that are interpretive. I think there are parts of the Bible that are allegorical. I think there are parts of the Bible that are meant to be interpreted in a modern context. So, yes, I believe it."

He has lots to say about the Bible. "I think it's the great [*sic*] book ever written. I read it frequently. I read it very frequently when I've gone through the bigger crises in my life, and I find great wisdom in it, and it does define to a very large extent my faith. But I don't believe every single thing in the literal sense of Jonah being in the belly of the whale, or, you know, there are some things in it that I think were put there as allegorical."[3]

While Giuliani claims that religion is important in his life, he acknowledges he's not the most devout Catholic and has had to fend off criticism of his religious sincerity.

While running for president in Iowa, Giuliani was asked if he considered himself a "traditional, practicing Roman Catholic." He replied, "My religious affiliation, my religious practices, and the degree to which I am a good or not so good Catholic, I prefer to leave to the priests," he said. "That would be a much better way to discuss it. That's a personal discussion, and they have a much better sense of how good a Catholic I am or how bad a Catholic I am."[4]

On another occasion when asked about his imperfect devotion, Giuliani shared the story of the adulterous woman who was being criticized and Jesus's reply in John 8:7, "He that is without sin among you, let him first cast a stone at her." He also shared his appreciation of Matthew 7:1. "I'm guided very, very often about, 'Don't judge others, lest you be judged,'" Giuliani said.

Faith, he declared, is "a very, very important part of my life. But I think in a democracy and in a government like ours, my religion is my way of looking at God, and other people have other ways of doing it, and some people don't believe in God," he said. "I think that's unfortunate. I think their life would be a lot fuller if they did, but they have that right."[5]

NOTES

1. "Outspoken Catholic Archbishop Raymond Burke Says He'd Deny Rudy Giuliani Communion," *Fox News*, 3 Oct 2007, http://www.foxnews.com/story/2007/10/03/outspoken-catholic-archbishop-raymond-burke-says-hed-deny-rudy-giuliani.html.

2. Barry Bearak and Ian Fisher, "RACE FOR CITY HALL: The Republican Candidate; A Mercurial Mayor's Confident Journey," *New York Times*, 19 Oct 1997, http://www.nytimes.com/1997/10/19/nyregion/race-for-city-hall-republican-candidate-mercurial-mayor-s-confident-journey.html?pagewanted=all.

3. "CNN/YouTube Republican Presidential Debate Transcript," *CNN*, 29 Nov 2007, http://www.cnn.com/2007/POLITICS/11/28/debate.transcript.part2/.

4. "Giuliani Questioned about His Catholicism," *NBC News*, 7 Aug 2007, http://www.nbcnews.com/id/20164315/ns/politics-decision_08/t/giuliani-questioned-about-his-catholicism/#.WbIihq2-LBI.

5. "Outspoken Catholic Archbishop."

31

AL GORE

Vice President of the United States

Discern the Sky and the Earth

And he said also to the people, When ye see a cloud rise out of the west, straightway ye say, There cometh a shower; and so it is.

And when ye see the south wind blow, ye say, There will be heat; and it cometh to pass.

Ye hypocrites, ye can discern the face of the sky and of the earth; but how is it that ye do not discern this time?

—Luke 12:54–56 (KJV)

A l Gore, son of a senator, longtime member of Congress, vice president under Bill Clinton, and the 2000 Democratic nominee for president, hailed from a Baptist family. He calls New Salem Missionary Baptist Church in Elmwood, Tennessee, his home church and was later baptized in Mt. Vernon Baptist Church in Arlington, Virginia. While he doesn't affiliate with the Southern Baptist Convention due to their lurch to the right, he still considers himself a Baptist. "I am a Christian. I am a Protestant. I am a Baptist," he explained to *Newsweek*.[1]

Like many religious Democrats, Gore has invoked the book of James in the New Testament. In a speech to the NAACP during the 2000 campaign against George W. Bush, he said, "Show me thy faith without thy works, and I will show thee my faith by my works"[2] (see James 2:17).

In his post–vice presidential activism on climate change, Gore, author of the award-winning book and documentary *An Inconvenient Truth*, has also cited the New Testament. In a speech to the climate action group Avaaz, he said, "From my faith tradition on the book of Luke, describing the words of Jesus," and he quoted Luke 12:54–56. He passionately called on his listeners to discern the earth today and act to stop climate change.[3]

NOTES

1. "Religious Background of Albert Gore, Jr.," *Adherents*, retrieved 27 Jun 2017, http://www .adherents.com/people/pg/Al_Gore.html.
2. Benedicta Cipolla, "'Faith without Works' Emerges as Democrats' Favorite Bible Verse," *Yada Yah*, 25 Jun 2008, http://forum.yadayahweh.com/default.aspx?g=posts&t=1020#post6554.
3. "Al Gore's Microphone Fails While He Uses Bible Verses to Push Global Warming," *InfoWars*, 18 Sep 2014, https://www.infowars.com/al-gores-microphone-fails-while-he-uses-bible-verses -to-push-global-warming/.

32

ULYSSES S. GRANT

Eighteenth President of the United States

The Spirit of the Lord Provides Wisdom

And there shall come forth a rod out of the stem of Jesse, and a Branch shall grow out of his roots:

And the spirit of the Lord shall rest upon him, the spirit of wisdom and understanding, the spirit of counsel and might, the spirit of knowledge and of the fear of the Lord;

And shall make him of quick understanding in the fear of the Lord: and he shall not judge after the sight of his eyes, neither reprove after the hearing of his ears.

—Isaiah 11:1–3 (KJV)

The hero general of the Civil War wasn't very fond of organized religion, but he did take stock in the Bible. "Hold fast to the Bible as the sheet anchor of your liberties," he wrote to the nation's children in the *Sunday School Times*. "Write its precepts in your hearts and practice them in your lives."[1]

It is uncertain which verses Grant wanted the Bible open to when he swore his affirmation in his first inaugural, but in his second inauguration in 1873, Grant chose the first three verses of Isaiah 11 (quoted above).[2]

These verses, prophesying of the coming Messiah, also seemed to tap into the Republican president's desire to have the spirit of wisdom and understanding, of knowledge, and of righteous judgments as he wrangled with the difficulties of Reconstruction and bringing a nation back together from the recent Civil War.

NOTES

1. John C. McCollister, *God and the Oval Office* (Nashville: W Publishing Group, 2005), 95. See also Art Farstad, "The Bible and the Presidents," *Faith Alone Magazine*, retrieved 21 Mar 2017, https://faithalone.org/magazine/y1992/92feb1.html.
2. Mahita Gajanan, "These Are the Bible Verses Past Presidents Have Turned to on Inauguration Day," *Time*, 19 Jan 2017, http://time.com/4639596/inauguration-day-presidents-bible-passages/.

33

COLLEEN HANABUSA

US Representative from Hawaii

All-Embracing Compassion

Whatever words we utter should be chosen with care, for people will hear them and be influenced by them for good or ill.

If one wishes to follow the Buddha's teaching one must not be egoistic or self-willed, but should cherish feeling of good-will toward all alike; one should respect those worthy of respect; one should serve those who are worthy of service and treat everyone with uniform kindness.

—*The Dharma, Gautama Buddha*

Hanabusa is a fourth-generation American of Japanese ancestry and became the third Buddhist ever elected to the US Congress. In fact, her election to return to Congress in 2016 after a brief absence made Hawaii the first state to ever have a non-Christian majority congressional delegation.

She is a devout member of the Waianae Hongwanji, a Buddhist temple in Waianae, Hawaii. The Hanabusa family was impactful in the founding of the temple. Her faith is an important part of her life, and she works to "integrate her Buddhist values into American political leadership."[1]

Congresswoman Hanabusa reveres the Three Treasures of Buddhism: the Buddha, the Dharma, and the Sangha. "May we all be guided and inspired by the Three Treasures," she said, pointing out that the teachings therein can especially help "those who are in leadership roles be reflective, open, thoughtful, wise, and compassionate in their endeavors."

At a bipartisan prayer service at St. Peter's Catholic Church in Washington, DC, in early 2017, Hanabusa shared some of her favorite verses from the Three Treasures. "The Buddha harbors no thought of greed, hatred or malice," she shared, "nor does the Buddha allow any ideas of greed, hatred, and malice to arise." She also shared Buddhist quotes from the Dharma on how to treat others with compassion (quoted above).

Finally, she offered words of the Sangha: "Thousands of people may live in a community but it is not a true community until all people know each other and have empathy for one another," the Democratic congresswoman shared. "A true community has faith and wisdom that illuminate it. It is place [sic] where people know and trust one another and where there is harmony."

Rep. Hanabusa concluded with her own Buddhist aspiration. "May the Light of All-Inclusive Wisdom and All-Embracing Compassion guide and illumine the hearts-and-minds of all people of all nations," she said, "so our thoughts, words, and actions may bring understanding, peace, harmony, and happiness, equally, to both self and others in our local, national and global communities!"[2]

Notes

1. "Buddhist Colleen Hanabusa Announces Senate Run," *Lions Roar: Buddhist Wisdom for Our Time*, 8 May 2013, https://www.lionsroar.com/buddhist-colleen-hanabusa-announces -senate-run.
2. "Buddhist Wisdom & Compassion Reaches Capitol Hill," *Honpa Hongwanji Mission of Hawaii*, 14 Jan 2017, http://hongwanjihawaii.com/blog/2017/01/14/buddhism-on-the-hill.

34

WARREN G. HARDING

Twenty-Ninth President of the United States

Justice, Mercy, Humility

He hath shewed thee, O man, what is good; and what doth the Lord require of thee, but to do justly, and to love mercy, and to walk humbly with thy God?

—*Micah 6:8 (KJV)*

It is my conviction that the fundamental trouble with the people of the United States is that they have gotten too far away from the Almighty God," Harding declared in 1920.[1] Not overly religious himself (he attended church regularly but always refused communion), he saw the value in the teachings of the Bible.

When being sworn in as president in 1921, Harding asked to borrow the same Bible used by George Washington, which belonged to St. John's Masonic Lodge No. 1. Harding was a mason, as was Washington. He had the book opened to the same verse Washington had quoted in his postwar letter to the governors of each state: Micah 6:8.[2]

After being sworn in on this scripture, the Republican from Ohio gave his address, concluding with referencing this verse he and the first president liked. "I have taken the solemn oath of office on that passage of Holy Writ wherein it is asked: 'What doth the Lord require of thee but to do justly, and to love mercy, and to walk humbly with thy God?' This I plight to God and country."[3]

NOTES

1. Quoted 16 Dec 2009 in the *Congressional Record*, House, Vol. 155, Pt. 24, p. 32543.
2. "The 34th Presidential Inauguration," Joint Congressional Committee on Inaugural Ceremonies, retrieved 11 Apr 2017, https://www.inaugural.senate.gov/about/past-inaugural -ceremonies/34th-inaugural-ceremonies/.
3. "Warren G. Harding Inaugural Address, 4 Mar 1921," *The American Presidency Project*, retrieved 13 Apr 2017, http://www.presidency.ucsb.edu/ws/?pid=25833.

35

KAMALA HARRIS

US Senator from California

Courage of Compassion

*Therefore, as God's chosen people, holy and dearly loved, clothe yourselves
with compassion, kindness, humility, gentleness and patience.*

—*Colossians 3:12 (NIV)*

The new junior senator from the Golden State was previously the state's
attorney general. As the daughter of immigrants, her father from Jamaica
and her mother from India, she is the second African-American female and
first Indian-American to serve in the United States Senate. "I grew up going
to a black Baptist Church and a Hindu temple," she said.[1]

Harris, who sang in the Baptist choir with her sister growing up, continues to feel comfortable in Christian churches.[2] In 2016, she spoke from
the pulpit of the Agape International Spiritual Center, Holman United
Methodist Church, and First African Methodist Episcopal Church. She
shared biblical verses and said the scriptures invite people "to speak up, judge
fairly, work for the needy."

"Think of the needy, the poor," she said at First AME. "Think of those who are vulnerable and voiceless, and when we do the right thing, speak on their behalf." The Democratic candidate went on, interpreting the scriptures, "And I think what we are being told also is that it is about having the courage of our compassion, especially in this environment when there seems to be far too little of it. And we are also being told to speak up, meaning pray and act."[3]

NOTES

1. Michael Finnegan, "How Race Helped Shape the Politics of Senate Candidate Kamala Harris," *Los Angeles Times,* 30 Sep 2015, http://www.latimes.com/local/politics/la-me-pol-ca-harris-senate-20150930-story.html.
2. Emily Bazelon, "Kamala Harris, a 'Top Cop' in the Era of Black Lives Matter," *New York Times,* 25 May 2016, https://www.nytimes.com/2016/05/29/magazine/kamala-harris-a-top-cop-in-the-era-of-black-lives-matter.html.
3. Christopher Cadelago, "Kamala Harris Merges Politics and Religion in Los Angeles," *Sacramento Bee,* 5 Jun 2016, http://www.sacbee.com/news/politics-government/capitol-alert/article81964427.html.

36

BENJAMIN HARRISON

Twenty-Third President of the United States

Lift Up Eyes to the Lord for Help

I will lift up mine eyes unto the hills, from whence cometh my help.
My help cometh from the Lord, which made heaven and earth.
He will not suffer thy foot to be moved: he that keepeth thee will
not slumber.
Behold, he that keepeth Israel shall neither slumber nor sleep.
The Lord is thy keeper: the Lord is thy shade upon thy right hand.
The sun shall not smite thee by day, nor the moon by night.

—Psalm 121:1–6 (KJV)

The grandson of President William Henry Harrison, Benjamin Harrison was a devout Presbyterian all his life. He taught Sunday School, was a church elder, and was known by the soldiers during the Civil War for saying nightly prayers in his tent.[1]

When winning the White House in 1888, he felt it an act of providence. When he stood on the East Portico of the Capitol to be sworn in, Harrison wanted to place his hand on the first six treasured verses from Psalm 121.[2]

"It is a great comfort to trust God—even if His providence is unfavorable," the Republican once wrote to a friend. "Prayer steadies one when he is walking in slippery places—even if things asked for are not given." As president, Harrison frequently encouraged the people to pray, and he urged the military to limit activities on the Sabbath. It was written of his time, "No morning is passed in the White House and no day's duties or pleasures are begun without the brief family prayer."[3]

NOTES

1. "God in the White House," *PBS*, retrieved 4 Apr 2017, http://www.pbs.org/godinamerica /god-in-the-white-house.
2. "The 26th Presidential Inauguration," Joint Congressional Committee on Inaugural Ceremonies, retrieved 11 Apr 2017, https://www.inaugural.senate.gov/about/past-inaugural -ceremonies/26th-inaugural-ceremonies.
3. "God in the White House."

37

WILLIAM HENRY HARRISON

Ninth President of the United States

Comforting Psalm on His Deathbed

Bless the Lord, O my soul: and all that is within me, bless his holy name.
Bless the Lord, O my soul, and forget not all his benefits. . . .
Bless the Lord, all his works in all places of his dominion: bless the
Lord, O my soul.

—Psalm 103 (KJV)

The ninth president was elected as a war hero—an Indian fighter that was the champion of the Battle of Tippecanoe. When he was sworn into office at the age of sixty-eight, Harrison tried to prove his manly vigor on a cold, windy day by not wearing a hat or coat. He not only gave the longest inaugural address in history (one hour, forty-five minutes), but he also rode a horse in the exposed weather throughout the inaugural parade.

The consequence of this machismo resulted in the new president catching a bad cold that turned into pneumonia. Thirty days later, President Harrison lay on his deathbed, never having recovered. He requested that the nurse attending him read aloud Psalm 103. A few minutes after the comforting verses were read, Harrison "closed his eyes and died peacefully."[1] The time this lover of Psalm 103 spent in office has gone down in history as the briefest presidential administration ever.

NOTE

1. John C. McCollister, *God and the Oval Office* (Nashville: W Publishing Group, 2005), 47.

38

ORRIN HATCH

US Senator from Utah

Lifelong Missionary

Adam fell that men might be; and men are, that they might have joy.
And the Messiah cometh in the fullness of time, that he may redeem
the children of men from the fall. And because that they are redeemed
from the fall they have become free forever, knowing good from evil; to
act for themselves and not to be acted upon, save it be by the punishment
of the law at the great and last day, according to the commandments
which God hath given.

—2 Nephi 2:25–26 (Book of Mormon)

O rrin Hatch is the longest-serving Republican senator in US history, and
due to his seniority, he was the President pro tempore of the United
States Senate and third in line to the presidency. He's also a lifelong man of
faith and student of the scriptures.

Descended from Letter-day Saint pioneers, Hatch was raised as a member
of The Church of Jesus Christ of Latter-day Saints, reading the scriptures and

saying family prayers daily. Still today he begins each day in the office by reading ten pages in the scriptures.[1]

"I had found the Lord at the age of seventeen" by reading the scriptures and praying about them, he said. "My commitment was total." Hatch attended the church's flagship school, Brigham Young University in Provo, Utah, which, coming from Pittsburgh where Latter-day Saints were a tiny minority, was a profound experience for him. "It was exciting to see people living Christian lives, and I really felt at home with them," he recalled.

At the age of twenty, Hatch left to serve a mission for his church, assigned to the Great Lakes Mission. For two years, he spread the gospel throughout Ohio, Michigan, and Indiana. Once, while Hatch and a missionary companion were knocking on doors in Springfield, Ohio, a large man answered the door with a revolver in his hand.

"I'm going to blow your head off," said the angry man as he pointed the gun in Hatch's face.

Despite panicking on the inside, Hatch boldly replied to the gunman, "We represent the Lord Jesus Christ," he said, "and if you pull the trigger, the gun will explode and kill you."

As the man lowered his firearm, Hatch and his companion backed away and then ran down the sidewalk. "I wasn't about to see if my prediction would come true," he said.[2]

Hatch later served as a bishop in his church, ministering to a congregation of six hundred, before launching his career in politics. Faith remained an important part of his life even in the Senate. In 1995, he began teaming up with Mormon Tabernacle Choir singer and prolific composer Janice Kapp Perry to write numerous songs, many of which captured his views of divinity. She would write the music, and Hatch would write the lyrics. They had titles such as "My God Is Love" and "My Dearest Savior," which lyrics include:

> *My dearest Savior / Who gently guides me / Into that kingdom / Free from all care,*
> *My dearest Savior / Thou art my guide star / Kindly persuading / Leading me there.*
> *My dearest Savior / When shall I see Thee? / I want to greet Thee / Free from all sin;*
> *My dearest Savior / Please stay beside me / Lead me through darkness / Bring me back home.*[3]

Ever the missionary, in 2012, Hatch published a book called *An American, A Mormon, and A Christian.* "People don't think Mormons are

Christian," he said. "That's totally wrong. [As a Mormon] you can hardly move without hearing the name of Jesus Christ. We're fervent believers in Jesus Christ."[4]

In the book, he shares many of his favorite scriptures, including the verses from 2 Nephi 2:25–26 in the Book of Mormon (quoted above) to explain his belief in Christ. "The gospel of Jesus Christ is true. I know that beyond any doubt and have expressed my testimony on many occasions to friendly and not-so-friendly audiences," he said. "Nothing else is as important as knowing that Jesus Christ atoned for our sins, died, was resurrected, and paved the way for us to return to our Father in Heaven with our families."[5]

NOTES

1. Lee Roderick, *Gentleman of the Senate: Orrin Hatch A Portrait of Character* (Washington, DC: Probitas Press, 2000), 11.
2. Ibid., 21.
3. Ibid., 271.
4. Elizabeth Flock, "Orrin Hatch on a Mission to Show Mormons Are Christians, Too," *U.S. News & World Report,* 10 Dec 2012, https://www.usnews.com/news/blogs/washington-whispers /2012/12/10/orrin-hatch-on-a-mission-to-show-mormons-are-christians-too.
5. Orrin Hatch, *An American, A Mormon, and a Christian: What I Believe* (Springville, UT: Plain Sight Publishing, 2012), 139. Book of Mormon verse quoted on page 33.

39

RUTHERFORD B. HAYES

Nineteenth President of the United States

The Lord Will Destroy Our Enemies

They compassed me about; yea, they compassed me about: but in the name of the Lord I will destroy them.

They compassed me about like bees; they are quenched as the fire of thorns: for in the name of the Lord I will destroy them.

Thou hast thrust sore at me that I might fall: but the Lord helped me.

—Psalm 118:11–13 (KJV)

The 1876 presidential election was one of the most contentious in American history. Democrat Samuel Tilden won the popular vote and initially seemed to have beaten the Republican candidate Hayes by one electoral vote. With twenty electoral votes produced under a dark cloud of suspicion, a bipartisan congressional commission was appointed to sort the mess out. Mere days before the March 4 inauguration day, Rutherford B. Hayes was declared the winner. His enemies were outraged and took to calling the new president "Rutherfraud" or "His Fraudulency."[1]

Perhaps it is because of this bitter time that Hayes selected the three verses of Psalm 118 (quoted above) to be sworn in on.[2] His enemies were indeed swarming about him like bees, needling him like a fire of thorns, and "thrust[ing] sore" at him. It is natural that he would cling to these verses of the Lord helping him and desiring to destroy his enemies.

Hayes wrote in his diary, "I belong to no church. But . . . I try to be a Christian, or rather I want to help to do Christian work." He and his devout Methodist wife held prayer readings at each breakfast and knelt and prayed aloud together the Lord's Prayer each morning. On Sunday evenings, they would invite other officials in the nation's capital over for hymn singing. Some of the president's favorite hymns were "Jesus, Lover of My Soul," "Blest Be the Tie That Binds," and "Nearer, My God, to Thee."[3]

Hayes embraced the teachings of the Bible. "The religion of the Bible is the best in the world," he wrote on another occasion in his diary. "I see the infinite value of religion. Let it be always encouraged."[4] Another time he wrote, "What a great mistake is made by him who does not support the religion of the Bible!"[5]

NOTES

1. Harry Barnard, *Rutherford Hayes and his America* (Newtown, CT: American Political Biography Press, 2005), 402–3.
2. Mahita Gajanan, "These Are the Bible Verses Past Presidents Have Turned to on Inauguration Day," *Time*, 19 Jan 2017, http://time.com/4639596/inauguration-day-presidents-bible-passages.
3. John C. McCollister, *God and the Oval Office* (Nashville: W Publishing Group, 2005), 99–100.
4. "God in the White House," *PBS*, retrieved 4 Apr 2017, http://www.pbs.org/godinamerica/god-in-the-white-house.
5. Rutherford B. Hayes, *Diary, Volume 4*, p. 168, retrieved 10 Apr 2017, http://apps.ohiohistory.org/hayes/index.php.

40

GARY HERBERT

Governor of Utah

Do Thou Likewise

Which now of these three, thinkest thou, was neighbour unto him that fell among the thieves?

And he said, He that shewed mercy on him. Then said Jesus unto him, Go, and do thou likewise.

—*Luke 10:36–37 (KJV)*

H erbert is an active member of The Church of Jesus Christ of Latter-day Saints. Like many Latter-day Saints, he served a two-year mission as a young man, in his case to proselyte in the eastern United States. He also attended the church's flagship school, Brigham Young University.

"We really ought to spend more time reading the scriptures," he said during an interfaith gathering at the Utah state capitol in 2013. "Regardless of our religious affiliation, the Bible provides us with a road map to heaven, to happiness, to how to conduct our lives," he said. "Like any good road map, the Bible can keep us from getting lost and can help us understand the directions we should take in our lives."

As part of this event, which was part of the National Bible Association's celebration of Salt Lake City as National Bible City 2013, Herbert shared his favorite scripture—the parable of the Good Samaritan found in Luke 10:25–37. After reading it, the Republican governor said, "This is a favorite scripture of mine because there was no government involvement in any part of the process here, and yet people were served very well because of the Good Samaritan."[1]

NOTE

1. Joseph Walker, "Governor, Others Gather for 'Joyful' Reading of Favorite Bible Verses," *Deseret News,* 25 Nov 2013, http://www.deseretnews.com/article/865591344/Governor-others-gather-for-joyful-reading-of-favorite-Bible-verses.html. See also Gary Herbert, "Governor Gary R Herbert: National Bible Day," *YouTube,* 25 Jun 2014, https://www.youtube.com/watch?v=09xMrJJO5PI.

41

MAZIE HIRONO

US Senator from Hawaii

Tolerance, Integrity, Honesty

Three things cannot be long hidden: the sun, the moon, and the truth.

—Buddha

History was made on January 6, 2007, when Mazie Hirono was sworn in as the first Buddhist member of the United States Congress. Born in Japan and reared in Honolulu, Hirono was raised Jōdo Shinshū, the most widely practiced form of Buddhism in Japan.[1]

Most members of the US House of Representatives were sworn in on a Bible that day. Her colleague Keith Ellison, a Democrat from Minnesota, was sworn in on Thomas Jefferson's Qur'an. Representative Hirono said, "I don't have a book, but I certainly believe in the precepts of Buddhism and that of tolerance of other religions and integrity and honesty."

Regarding the controversy swirling around Ellison and the Qur'an, Hirono said, "It's about time that we have people of other backgrounds and faiths in Congress." She continued, "What happened to separation of church and state and religious tolerance? I believe in those things."[2]

After six years in the House, in 2013, Hirono was sworn in as the junior senator from Hawaii, becoming the first Buddhist in the upper chamber of Congress. She is also the first Asian American female in the Senate. Hirono encourages harmony and peace in addressing the nation's issues. "The way in which we solve our problems will determine how lasting our ability to work together will be," the Buddhist Senator once said at a Hawaii Prayer Breakfast.[3]

NOTES

1. "Buddhists Get the Vote," *Manitoba Buddhist Temple,* 5 Nov 2010, http://www.manitoba buddhistchurch.org/blog_files/category-usa.html.
2. Dennis Camire, "Buddhist congresswoman sworn in, urges tolerance," *Buddhist Channel,* 6 Jan 2007, http://www.buddhistchannel.tv/index.php?id=60,3603,0,0,1,0#.WUYPhZIrLIU.
3. Mary Adamski, "Strikes, spy plane top prayer agenda," *Honolulu Star-Bulletin,* 7 Apr 2001, http://archives.starbulletin.com/2001/04/07/news/story21.html.

42

HERBERT HOOVER

Thirty-First President of the United States

Keepeth the Law

Where there is no vision, the people perish: but he that keepeth the law, happy is he.

—*Proverbs 29:18 (KJV)*

H oover was a Quaker, and as a boy he went to church each Sunday, where he read the Bible, as he describes, "in daily stints from cover to cover." He wrote of the Bible, "As a nation we are indebted to the Book of Books for our national ideals and representative institutions. Their preservation rests in adhering to its principles."[1]

When inaugurated in March 1929, the new president was soaking wet from the downpour, yet he was forward-looking in that rain and ensured that the family Bible he affirmed the oath on be opened to Proverbs 29:18. Exuding the vision and optimism of that verse in his inaugural address, Hoover declared, "I have no fears for the future of our country. It is bright with hope."[2]

However, the stock market crash of seven months later ushered in the Great Depression and a time of great difficulty for President Hoover and the nation. Still, he clung to the words of the "Book of Books," as he called it.

"Whether it be of the law, business, morals, or that vision which leads the imagination in the creation of constructive enterprises for the happiness of mankind," the Republican declared, "he who looks for guidance in any of these things may look inside its covers and find illumination."[3]

NOTES

1. "God in the White House," *PBS*, retrieved 4 Apr 2017, http://www.pbs.org/godinamerica /god-in-the-white-house.
2. "The 36th Presidential Inauguration," Joint Congressional Committee on Inaugural Ceremonies, retrieved 11 Apr 2017, https://www.inaugural.senate.gov/about/past-inaugural -ceremonies/36th-inaugural-ceremonies.
3. Art Farstad, "The Bible and the Presidents," *Faith Alone Magazine*, retrieved 21 Mar 2017, https://faithalone.org/magazine/y1992/92feb1.html.

43

MIKE HUCKABEE

Governor of Arkansas

Perfected in Christ

And He has said to me, "My grace is sufficient for you, for power is perfected in weakness." Most gladly, therefore, I will rather boast about my weaknesses, so that the power of Christ may dwell in me.

—*2 Corinthians 12:9 (New American Standard Bible)*

The former governor of Arkansas, Republican presidential candidate, and television personality began his career as a pastor. Mike Huckabee was a staffer for televangelist James Robison at age twenty-one. From 1980 to 1986, he was the pastor at Immanuel Baptist Church in Pine Bluff, Arkansas, and from 1986 to 1992, he was the pastor at Beech Street First Baptist Church in Texarkana. During that time, he also had a term as president of the Arkansas Baptist State Convention.

This time as a pastor gave him insights into how faith impacts people on a day-to-day basis. "I was in the ICU at 2 a.m. with families faced with the decision to disconnect a respirator on their loved one," he said. "I counseled fifteen-year-old pregnant girls who were afraid to tell their parents about their condition; I spent hours hearing the grief of women who had been physically and emotionally clobbered by an abusive husband; I saw the anguish in the faces of an elderly couple when their declining health forced them to sell their home, give up their independence, and move into a long-term-care facility; I listened to countless young couples pour out their souls as they struggled to get their marriages into survival mode when confronted with overextended debt."[1]

He has long loved the Bible. "I believe the Bible is exactly what it is," he said. "It's the word of revelation to us from God himself. I don't fully comprehend and understand it all, because the Bible is a revelation of an infinite god, and no finite person is ever going to fully understand it. If they do, their god is too small."[2]

The biblical themes of faith and redemption strongly resonate with Huckabee. "I make no apology for my faith. My faith explains me," he said in a 2008 interview on *Meet the Press*. "It means that I believe that we're all frail, it means that we're all fragile, that all of us have faults, none of us are perfect, that all of us need redemption."[3]

Huckabee later elaborated on the role Jesus Christ plays in that redemption. He takes literally the scripture in Matthew 5:48 (NASB), "Therefore you are to be perfect, as your heavenly Father is perfect," but he also believes that Christ can make up the difference.

"The criteria to get into heaven is you have to be not good, but perfect. That's the real challenge in it," he explained in a 2008 interview. "On that day, when I pull up, I'll be asked, 'Do you have what it takes to get in?' And if I ask, 'Well, what does it take to get in?' 'Gotta be perfect.' 'Well, I'm afraid I don't have that,' but you know what, I won't be there alone that day. Somebody is going to be with me. His name is Jesus, and he's promised that he would never leave me or forsake me."

Huckabee loves the biblical verses about grace and about Jesus Christ helping us fill in the gaps in our heavenly quest for perfection, such as the verse from 2 Corinthians quoted above. "I have deep convictions about who goes [to heaven] and who doesn't," Huckabee said, "but as far as who makes that decision, it isn't me, it's God. I'm going to leave that up to him."[4]

NOTES

1. Mike Huckabee, *From Hope to Higher Ground* (New York: Center Street, 2007), 7.
2. "32 Mike Huckabee Quotes," *Christian Quotes*, accessed 30 Aug 2017, https://www .christianquotes.info/quotes-by-author/mike-huckabee-quotes/#axzz4ZCIaseq5.
3. "Meet the Press Transcript for Jan. 28, 2007," *NBC News*, http://www.nbcnews.com /id/16785556/page/2/#.WacaDq2-LBI.

4. "Mike Huckabee on God's Judgments about Who Gets into Heaven," *Berkley Center for Religion, Peace & World Affairs, Georgetown University,* 13 Jan 2008, https://berkleycenter .georgetown.edu/quotes/mike-huckabee-on-god-s-judgments-about-who-gets-into-heaven.

44

ANDREW JACKSON

Seventh President of the United States

Judge the Trees by Their Fruits

A good tree cannot bring forth evil fruit, neither can a corrupt tree bring forth good fruit.

Every tree that bringeth not forth good fruit is hewn down, and cast into the fire.

Wherefore by their fruits ye shall know them.

—Matthew 7:18–20 (KJV)

I was brought up a rigid Presbyterian, to which I have always adhered," Jackson wrote in 1835. "Our excellent Constitution guarantees to every one freedom of religion, and charity tells us (and you know charity is the real basis of all true religion) . . . judge the tree by its fruit." Jackson believed in those words found in Matthew.

"All who profess Christianity believe in a Savior, and that by and through Him we must be saved," he wrote. "We ought, therefore, to consider all good Christians whose walks correspond with their professions, be they Presbyterian, Episcopalian, Baptist, Methodist, or Roman Catholic."[1]

Jackson claimed in his diary to read three to five chapters from the Bible each day. "Go read the Scriptures," he once wrote to a son-in-law. "The joyful promises it contains will be balsam to all your troubles."[2]

When someone once belittled the Bible, the seventh president shot back, "That book, Sir, is the Rock upon which our republic rests."[3]

NOTES

1. Bill Federer, "Bible: 'The Rock upon Which Our Republic Rests.'" *World Net Daily*, 7 Jun 2015, http://www.wnd.com/2015/06/bible-the-rock-upon-which-our-republic-rests.
2. John C. McCollister, *God and the Oval Office* (Nashville: W Publishing Group, 2005), 39.
3. Federer, "Bible."

45

THOMAS JEFFERSON

Third President of the United States

Disciple of the Doctrines of Jesus

Blessed are the peacemakers: for they shall be called the children of God.

—*Matthew 5:9 (KJV)*

The third president loved the teachings of Jesus of Nazareth but felt that His true essence was buried underneath embellishments to His life story by disciples after His death. Of "the corruptions of Christianity, I am indeed opposed," Jefferson wrote to Benjamin Rush. "But not to the genuine precepts of Jesus himself. I am a Christian, in the only sense in which he wished any one to be; sincerely attached to his doctrines, in preference to all others; ascribing to himself every human excellence, [and] believing he never claimed any other."[1]

So, with a sharp razor and glue, he cut and pasted the verses he liked, omitted stories that offended his reason, and left on the floor any account of miracles. He bound the eighty-four-page volume in red leather and called it *The Life and Morals of Jesus of Nazareth Extracted Textually from the Gospels in Greek, Latin, French and English.*[2]

Stephen Prothero, a religion professor at Boston University, called it "scripture by subtraction."[3] It was clear which teachings Jefferson still revered as scripture. The Beatitude quoted above from Matthew, for example, was kept in all four languages in this "Jefferson Bible."

As a result of this thorough—and unique—scripture study, Jefferson felt satisfied in his final years calling himself "a real Christian, that is to say, a disciple of the doctrines of Jesus."[4]

NOTES

1. "Jefferson's Religious Beliefs," *Monticello Official Site,* retrieved 21 Sep 2017, https://www .monticello.org/site/research-and-collections/jeffersons-religious-beliefs.
2. Marilyn Mellowes, "Thomas Jefferson and His Bible," *Frontline: From Jesus to Christ,* retrieved 4 Apr 2017, http://www.pbs.org/wgbh/pages/frontline/shows/religion/jesus/jefferson.html.
3. Owen Edwards, "How Thomas Jefferson Created His Own Bible," *Smithsonian Magazine, January 2012,* retrieved 4 Apr 2017, http://www.smithsonianmag.com/arts-culture/how -thomas-jefferson-created-his-own-bible-5659505/?all.
4. "God in the White House," *PBS,* retrieved 4 Apr 2017, http://www.pbs.org/godinamerica /god-in-the-white-house.

46

ANDREW JOHNSON

Seventeenth President of the United States

Faith in Battling Strong Drink

Wine is a mocker, strong drink is raging: and whosoever is deceived thereby is not wise. . . .

The king's heart is in the hand of the Lord, as the rivers of water: he turneth it whithersoever he will.

—Proverbs 20:1; 21:1 (KJV)

Hannibal Hamblin was Lincoln's first vice president, but for his second term Lincoln chose a southern Democrat, Andrew Johnson, to demonstrate hope for the national union in the closing days of the Civil War. On the day of Lincoln's second inaugural, Vice President Johnson was sworn in first, inside the Capitol in the Senate chambers. He showed up hung over from drinking the night before, drank a little whiskey before the event, and then rambled on for a seventeen-minute speech. "Do not let Johnson speak outside!" ordered Lincoln as the party went outside for his swearing in.

Six weeks later, Lincoln was assassinated. When Vice President Johnson was informed, he was in a drunken sleep, and his friends struggled to wake him. A doctor and a barber were brought in to help clean him up and prepare him for his ten o'clock swearing in ceremony.[1]

Perhaps it was because of his struggle with drink that Johnson had the Bible turned to Proverbs 20 and 21 before he put his left hand on it for the inauguration.[2] It seemed as if he were reaching out to the heavens in humility for help in the new, heavy responsibility.

NOTES

1. "Presidents Behaving Badly: Andrew Johnson's Drunken Inauguration," *Presidential History Geeks,* 6 Mar 2016, http://potus-geeks.livejournal.com/692889.html.
2. Mahita Gajanan, "These Are the Bible Verses Past Presidents Have Turned to on Inauguration Day," *Time,* 19 Jan 2017, http://time.com/4639596/inauguration-day-presidents-bible-passages.

47

HANK JOHNSON

US Representative from Georgia

Action for Peace

Nam-myoho-renge-kyo
(Devotion to the Mystic Law of the Lotus Sutra)

—*Nichiren's Buddhist chant*

It is a remarkable testament to the plurality of America's civic life that there are three Buddhists in Congress and that one of them is an African-American lawyer from Georgia. Rep. Hank Johnson, a Democrat, is relatively quiet about his religion. He "considers it a private matter," said a spokeswoman. "He will not give interviews on his faith."[1]

Another spokesperson, however, said, "Johnson would only confirm that he became a Buddhist some thirty years ago and is affiliated with Soka Gakkai International."[2] There are over one hundred thousand members of Soka Gakkai in the United States—15 percent are African-American—and some are high-profile converts, like musician Tina Turner and actors Patrick Duffy and Orlando Bloom.

Soka Gakkai (translated as "Society for the Creation of Value") was founded in Japan in 1930 as a form of Nichiren Buddhism. "The core Buddhist practice of SGI members is chanting Nam-myoho-renge-kyo and reciting portions of the Lotus Sutra, and sharing the teachings of Buddhism with others in order to help them overcome their problems," according to the official website of Soka Gakkai International.

"The practice of chanting Nam-myoho-renge-kyo was established by Nichiren (1222–82), a reformist Buddhist monk who identified the Lotus Sutra as the core teaching of Shakyamuni Buddha," the site said.[3]

When recited over and over, the phrase, which translates to "Devotion to the Mystic Law of the Lotus Sutra," is thought to bring good karma, eradicate negative karma, reduce sufferings, and bring a complete and perfect awakening. Twice daily, members of Soka Gakkai, like Johnson, chant the phrase Nam-myoho-renge-kyo for fifteen to twenty minutes while seated before a Buddhist mandala or shrine. It is also common for them to recite parts of the Lotus Sutra.[4]

Johnson's friend and fellow practitioner Sam Harris said that when they first joined the faith thirty years ago they would chant for material things. "In the beginning, I was chanting to somehow get me a car," he said. "Today, the things I chant for are other members' growth and development. And for some kind of solution for the war in Iraq." The sacred phrase Nam-myoho-renge-kyo is an important verse in Representative Johnson's spirituality.[5]

NOTES

1. Daniel Burke, "Diversity and a Buddhist Sect," *Washington Post*, 24 Feb 2007, http://www.washingtonpost.com/wp-dyn/content/article/2007/02/23/AR2007022301394.html.
2. "Hank Johnson," *The Mahablog*, 24 Dec 2006, http://www.mahablog.com/2006/12/24/hank-johnson.
3. Soka Gakkai International website, retrieved Jun 4, 2017, http://www.sgi.org/about-us/daily-practice.html.
4. Burke, "Diversity and a Buddhist Sect."
5. Ibid.

48

LYNDON B. JOHNSON

Thirty-Sixth President of the United States

Let Us Reason Together

Come now, and let us reason together, saith the Lord.

—Isaiah 1:18 (KJV)

Johnson had an ecumenical streak to his religion. After all, his mother was a Baptist, he was raised in the Disciples of Christ, and his wife, Lady Bird, was an Episcopalian. His father's favorite Bible verse was adopted as his, too: "Come now, and let us reason together."

Later as a member of the House of Representatives, as a senator (including six years as Senate Majority Leader), and then as president, Johnson would put his long arm around a colleague and invoke that verse in his efforts to generate support for legislation.

"Johnson's goal as president was to achieve consensus—to occupy that common ground on which the general citizenry and Congress alike could stand with him," it is remembered of the Democratic president. "One of his favorite sayings, 'Come, let us reason together,' became a rallying call to his banner."[1]

The Constitutional Rights Foundation noted, "Lyndon Johnson was a master of compromise. His ability to convince congressional adversaries to 'reason together' enabled Johnson to push controversial legislation through Congress."[2]

Johnson also quoted King Solomon's prayer from 2 Chronicles 1:10 at the end his inaugural address. "For myself, I ask only, in the words of an ancient leader: 'Give me now wisdom and knowledge, that I may go out and come in before this people: for who can judge this thy people, that is so great?'"[3]

NOTES

1. "Lyndon B. Johnson—Consensus politics," *Profiles of U.S. Presidents,* retrieved 29 Apr 2017, http://www.presidentprofiles.com/Kennedy-Bush/Lyndon-B-Johnson-Consensus-politics .html.

2. "Let Us Reason Together: Lyndon Johnson, Master Legislator," *Constitutional Rights Foundation*, retrieved 29 Apr 2017, http://www.crf-usa.org/bill-of-rights-in-action/bria-9-3 -and-4-a-let-us-reason-together-lyndon-johnson-master-legislator.html.

3. "The 45th Presidential Inauguration," Joint Congressional Committee on Inaugural Ceremonies, retrieved 11 Apr 2017, https://www.inaugural.senate.gov/about/past-inaugural -ceremonies/45th-inaugural-ceremonies/.

49

SAM JOHNSON

US Congressman from Texas

Strength from the Eternal

So we fix our eyes not on what is seen, but on what is unseen, since what is seen is temporary, but what is unseen is eternal.

—*2 Corinthians 4:18 (NIV)*

J ohnson is a lifelong Methodist and a graduate of Southern Methodist University. He spent twenty-nine years in the Unites States Air Force, flying missions in both the Korean and Vietnam Wars. A defining point in his journey of faith was the trial of seven years as a prisoner of war in Hanoi during the Vietnam War, spending nearly half the time in solitary confinement.

"Through it all, one lesson still strikes clearly," he said. "The scriptures say, 'We fix our eyes not on what is seen, but on what is unseen, since what is seen is temporary, but what is unseen is eternal.'

"With a body broken by my captors, but alive with the Holy Spirit, I can share a vivid testimony for Christ. Thanks to His handiwork, I have found it easy to make friends of faith on Capitol Hill," the Republican congressman said.

"I humbly thank God for every wonderful blessing in my life, including the blessing of *freedom* and that I can call America *home*.[1]

NOTE

1. Virginia Foxx, *God Is in the House: Congressional Testimonies of Faith* (Salt Lake City: Ensign Peak, 2016), 36.

50

TIM KAINE

US Senator from Virginia

Humility of Mind

Do nothing from selfishness or empty conceit, but with humility of mind regard one another as more important than yourselves.

—*Philippians 2:3 (NASB)*

Tim Kaine, mayor of Richmond, governor of Virginia, senator, and Hillary Clinton's vice presidential running mate, attended a Jesuit high school growing up. He latched onto the school's motto, "Men for others," and volunteered for nine months with missionaries in Honduras. Today, he and his wife are congregants of the St. Elizabeth Catholic Church in Richmond.

Of himself and Clinton, he said, "We share this basic belief. It's simple. Do all the good you can and serve one another. Pretty simple."[1]

During the heat of the 2016 campaign, Donald Trump said on MSNBC that women should be punished for having abortions. In the subsequent vice presidential debate, it was a gaffe that Kaine jumped on. "From the fullness of the heart, the mouth speaks," the Democrat said. "When Donald Trump says that women should be punished, or Mexicans are criminals, or John McCain's not a hero, he is showing you who he is."[2]

The line "from the fullness of the heart, the mouth speaks" is a paraphrase of both Luke 6:45 and Matthew 15:18. "A good man out of the good treasure of his heart bringeth forth that which is good . . . for of the abundance of the heart his mouth speaketh," said Luke. "But those things which proceed out of the mouth come forth from the heart; and they defile the man," said Matthew.

In an August 2016 appearance on the Late Show with Stephen Colbert, Kaine was asked what his favorite scripture was. He shared Philippians 2:3 (quoted above) and expressed the importance of humility. Kaine shared about being a Jesuit missionary and always appreciating Paul's admonitions to the Philippians to look beyond themselves. He said this was something he tried to do in his public service.[3]

NOTES

1. Benjamin Wallace-Wells, "Tim Kaine Takes Back Faith for the Democrats," *New Yorker,* 28 Jul 2016, http://www.newyorker.com/news/benjamin-wallace-wells/tim-kaine-takes-back -faith-for-the-democrats.
2. Dan Andros, "Here's the Bible Verse Kaine Used to Slam Trump," *FaithWire,* 5 Oct 2016, http://www.faithwire.com/2016/10/05/heres-the-bible-verse-kaine-used-to-slam-trump.
3. "The Late Show with Stephen Colbert," 25 Aug 2016, https://www.cbs.com/shows/the-late -show-with-stephen-colbert/video/1FC4197D-B421-9B8F-9CAC-C49C992EC2F0/tim -kaine-recalls-that-fateful-call-from-hillary-clinton.

51

JOHN KASICH

Governor of Ohio

Judgment Is God's

Or how can you say to your brother, "Let me take the speck out of your eye," and behold, the log is in your own eye?

You hypocrite, first take the log out of your own eye, and then you will see clearly to take the speck out of your brother's eye.

—*Matthew 7:4–5 (NASB)*

The governor of Ohio is a former member of Congress and was a 2016 Republican presidential candidate. The child of immigrants, Kasich grew up "a card-carrying Catholic" in "working-class church-abiding" McKees Rocks, Pennsylvania.[1] Aspiring to be the best altar boy in his parish, Kasich was devout and earned the nickname "Pope" from his friends.[2]

"I drifted away from religion as a young adult," Kasich wrote. "Then I looked up one day, and there was a huge hole in my life where God and religion had been." This was made especially acute after his parents were killed by a drunk driver. "I wanted to know if this 'God thing' was real," he said, so he joined a weekly Bible study reform group after his parents' death.[3]

That experience proved to be so profound for him, Kasich wrote a book about it, *Every Other Monday: Twenty Years of Life, Lunch, Faith, and Friendship.* Since then, he's felt God with him and become well versed in the Bible, often quoting it in his public life. "He's with me wherever I happen to be," he said. "I find God in the stories of the Bible, in the random acts of kindness I see every day, in the choices I make and the ways I interact."

The stories of the Bible became real to him. "I believe there was indeed an ark—and not just any ark but an impossibly, unfathomably huge ark—and that Noah undertook this impossibly, unfathomably huge task and completed it heroically."[4]

He cites the New Testament when saying why Ohio should expand Medicaid. "I mention Matthew 25," Kasich admits. "It really rankles people, but that's okay. I'm playing for a bigger game. We have to pay attention to the widowed and the poor. People say there's another way to do it, and I say, 'Fine, then do it.' I'd rather not have the government have to do all these things, but if nobody's going to do anything about it and if the problem is so big the government needs to be somewhat involved, I'm not going to look the other way and think those people don't exist, because they *can* get on their feet. Everyone has a God-given purpose, and I want that God-given purpose to be carried out or fulfilled."[5]

Kasich is also cautious about judging people. "There's a wonderful adage in the Bible: 'Don't judge another person when he has a speck in his eye, because you have a log in your own.'" He continued, "I read a line like that and set it alongside the stuff of my life and come to the conclusion that judgment is not our job. It's God's job to sort that stuff out."

He continues on judgment: "And let's not forget that justice doesn't always happen here on earth. When we think in our minds that somebody is getting away with something he shouldn't or that a certain punishment wasn't severe enough to fit the crime, we get frustrated. Sometimes we see justice on this side of the grave, but I have the faith to believe that the ultimate judge, the highest judge, will bring justice in the long run."[6]

Today, he is a member of the Anglican Church of St. Augustine in Westerville, Ohio, which is part of the conservative Anglican Church in North America.

NOTES

1. Cathy Lynn Grossman, "5 Faith Facts about Gov. John Kasich: 'God Is with Me Wherever I Happen to Be,'" *Washington Post,* 21 Jul 2015, https://www.washingtonpost.com/national /religion/5-faith-facts-about-gov-john-kasich-god-is-with-me-wherever-i-happen-to-be

/2015/07/21/03e8a768-2fbb-11e5-a879-213078d03dd3_story.html?utm_term=
.21a44leedcc2.

2. Laura Turner, "How Kasich's Religion Is Hurting Him with Conservatives," *Politico,* 15 Mar
    2016, http://www.politico.com/magazine/story/2016/03/john-kasich-2016-religion-213735.

3. Peter-Michael Preble, "The Faith of John Kasich," *Huffington Post,* 11 Mar 2017, http://www
    .huffingtonpost.com/fr-petermichael-preble/the-faith-of-john-kasich_b_9413406.html.

4. Grossman, "5 Faith Facts about Gov. John Kasich."

5. David Brody, "John Kasich, The Bible And Medicaid," *CBN News,* 22 Jun 2015, http://www1
    .cbn.com/thebrodyfile/archive/2015/06/22/john-kasich-the-bible-and-medicaid.

6. John Kasich, *Every Other Monday: Twenty Years of Life, Lunch, Faith, and Friendship* (New
    York: Atria Books, 2010), 212.

52

JOHN F. KENNEDY

Thirty-Fifth President of the United States

A Time for Everything

There is an appointed time for everything, and a time for every affair under the heavens.

A time to be born and a time to die. A time to plant, and a time to uproot the plant.

A time to kill, and a time to heal. A time to tear down, and a time to build.

A time to weep, and a time to laugh. A time to mourn, and a time to dance.

A time to scatter stones, and a time to gather them. A time to embrace, and a time to be far from embraces.

A time to seek, and a time to lose. A time to keep, and a time to cast away.

A time to rend, and a time to sew. A time to be silent, and a time to speak.

A time to love, and a time to hate. A time of war, and a time of peace.

—*Ecclesiastes 3:1–8 (New American Bible)*

President John Kennedy was fond of quoting the Holy Bible," declared Kennedy's friend and spiritual advisor Archbishop Philip Hannan in his funeral eulogy. When he accepted the Democratic nomination for president, Kennedy fused together two Old Testament prophets in his remarks.

"Be strong and of good courage. Be not afraid, neither be thou dismayed," he said, quoting Joshua 1:9. "They that wait upon the Lord shall renew their strength. They shall mount up with wings as eagles. They shall run and not be weary," he said, pulling from Isaiah 40:31.

Hannan pointed out that the president quoted Luke 9:62 while speaking to the United Nations just two months before he was killed. "Let us complete what we have started," Kennedy said, "for as the Scriptures tell us, no man who puts his hand to the plow and looks back is fit for the kingdom of God."

The previous Thursday at what would be the final dinner of America's first Catholic president, Hannan reported, Kennedy referenced Joel 2:28 ("Your old men shall dream dreams, your young men shall see visions.") and Proverbs 29:18 ("And where there is no vision the people perish.").

Archbishop Hannan said that Kennedy's speech in Dallas, which he did not live to deliver, referenced Psalm 127:1, the verse also liked by President John Quincy Adams. "The righteousness of our cause must always underlie our strength," he was to say, "for as was written long ago: 'Except the Lord guard the city, the guard watches in vain.'"

Yet after pointing out these scripture references used by the late president on occasions that seemed to fit, Hannan declared that in a general sense "one of his favorite passages from Scripture" was the first eight verses of Ecclesiastes chapter three.[1] These verses (quoted above) were provided to Hannan from the Kennedy family, and when Archbishop Hannan read those verses at the funeral about how all things happen in God's time, he heard many of the congregation sobbing.[2]

NOTES

1. "John F. Kennedy Funeral Eulogy Cited Slain President's Favorite Bible Passages," *Huffington Post*, 22 Nov 2013, http://www.huffingtonpost.com/2013/11/22/john-f-kennedy-funeral-eulogy_n_4309994.html.
2. Mark Zimmerman, "Memoir recalls bishop setting aside own grief to write Kennedy eulogy," *National Catholic Reporter*, 22 Nov 2013, https://www.ncronline.org/news/people/memoir-recalls-bishop-setting-aside-own-grief-write-kennedy-eulogy.

53

JOHN KERRY

US Secretary of State

Faith Requires Works

What good is it, my brothers, if someone says he has faith but does not have works? Can that faith save him? . . .
    So also faith by itself, if it does not have works, is dead.

—*James 2:14, 17 (English Standard Version)*

John Kerry's father was a Catholic and his mother was an Episcopalian, but he was raised Catholic. "I thought of being a priest. I was very religious while at school in Switzerland," he said. "I was an altar boy and prayed all the time. I was very centered around the Mass and the church."

He has continued to be very religious as an adult. Kerry is known to always carry a prayer book and a St. Christopher medal (patron saint of travelers), and he insists on attending Mass even when traveling. Kerry has a connection with Jesus, he says, which he accesses through his relationship with Mary, the Lord's mother, when he prays the rosary.

Kerry said he has been moved by the letters of Paul, which "taught [him] not to feel sorry for [him]self." He has also invoked numerous other scriptures in his public speeches, including the commandment to "love thy neighbor as thyself." He said, "The second commandment means that our commitment to equal rights and social justice, here and around the world, is not simply a matter of political fashion or economic and social theory but a direct command from God."[1]

While running for president in 2004, the Democratic nominee referenced the book of James. "There's a great passage of the Bible that says, 'What does it mean my brother to say you have faith if there are no deeds? Faith without works is dead,'" he said, paraphrasing James 2:14 and 17.

"And I think that everything you do in public life has to be guided by your faith, affected by your faith, but without transferring it in any official way to other people," he continued. "That's why I fight against poverty. That's why I fight to clean up the environment and protect this earth. That's why I fight for equality and justice."[2]

As Secretary of State, he referenced Genesis in a speech on US-Muslim relations. "Confronting climate change is, in the long run, one of the greatest challenges that we face, and you can see this duty or responsibility laid out in Scriptures clearly, beginning in Genesis," he said. "And Muslim-majority countries are among the most vulnerable. Our response to this challenge ought to be rooted in a sense of stewardship of Earth, and for me and for many of us here today, that responsibility comes from God," Kerry said.[3]

In speaking to an AME Convention, Kerry invoked Ecclesiastes 3:3. "Scripture tells us there is 'a time to break down and a time to build up,'" he said. "This is our time to break down division and build up unity. This is our time to reject the politics of fear."[4]

NOTES

1. "Not a Prodigal Son," *Beliefnet*, retrieved 26 Jun 2017, http://www.beliefnet.com/news /politics/2004/08/not-a-prodigal-son.aspx?.
2. Benedicta Cipolla, "'Faith without works' emerges as Democrats' favorite Bible verse," *Yada Yah*, 25 Jun 2008, http://forum.yadayahweh.com/default.aspx?g=posts&t=1020#post6554.
3. "Kerry: Scripture Says U.S. Should Protect Muslim Countries Against Global Warming," *Washington Free Beacon*, 3 Sep 2014, http://freebeacon.com/issues/kerry-scripture-says-u-s -should-protect-muslim-countries-against-global-warming.
4. "John Kerry on Faith," *Beliefnet*, retrieved 26 Jun 2017, http://www.beliefnet.com/news /politics/2004/07/john-kerry-on-faith.aspx.

54

DENNIS KUCINICH

US Representative from Ohio

An Instrument of Peace

Lord, make me an instrument of Your peace. Where there is hatred, let me sow love; where there is injury, pardon; where there is doubt, faith; where there is despair, hope; where there is darkness, light; where there is sadness, joy.

O, Divine Master, grant that I may not so much seek to be consoled as to console; to be understood as to understand; to be loved as to love; For it is in giving that we receive; it is in pardoning that we are pardoned; it is in dying that we are born again to eternal life.

—Prayer by St. Francis

Dennis Kucinich, at age thirty-one, was the youngest mayor of a major American city when elected to lead Cleveland, Ohio, in 1977. He later served in the Ohio State Senate and the US House of Representatives, and he was a candidate for the Democratic presidential nomination in both 2004 and 2008.

Before the age of seventeen, Kucinich had lived in twenty-one different places, including an orphanage and a car. He was raised in a Roman Catholic family, and he and his family attended Mass at more than a dozen churches. He also attended St. John Cantius School, a Catholic high school in Cleveland. Kucinich "studied the Scriptures and the lives of the saints, and was influenced by the Catholic Workers Movement." This background, he said, inspires him to "live each day with a grateful heart and a desire to be of service to humanity."[1]

He is currently a member of St. Aloysius Church in Cleveland. When asked in a 2007 presidential debate to name his favorite scripture, the Catholic congressman replied, "Prayer from St. Francis, which says, 'Lord make me an instrument of your peace.'"[2] This makes sense, coming from a candidate who gave an inspiring speech called "A Prayer for America" and was known for his efforts in public service, peace, human rights, workers' rights, and the environment.

NOTES

1. "Religion and Politics '08: Dennis Kucinich," *Pew Research Center,* 4 Nov 2008, http://www.pewforum.org/2008/11/04/religion-and-politics-08-dennis-kucinich.
2. Jeff Zeleny, "The Democrats Quote Scripture," *New York Times*, 27 Sep 2007, https://thecaucus.blogs.nytimes.com/2007/09/27/the-democrats-quote-scripture.

55

MARY LANDRIEU

US Senator from Louisiana

Wings as Eagles

But they that wait upon the Lord shall renew their strength; they shall mount up with wings as eagles; they shall run, and not be weary; and they shall walk, and not faint.

—Isaiah 40:31 (KJV)

A devout Roman Catholic since her childhood, Mary Landrieu attended Ursuline Academy, a private, all-girls Catholic school in New Orleans. Often attacked for her pro-choice views on abortion, Landrieu, a Democrat, touted her Catholicism in debates and throughout her campaigns to attempt to connect with voters of faith.

On election night in November 2014, which sent her into a runoff, she buoyed her supporters with a Bible verse in her speech: "You know one of my favorite scriptures is Isaiah 40:31. 'But they that wait upon the Lord shall renew their strength. They shall mount up with wings as eagles. They shall run and not be weary. They shall walk and not faint.'"[1] Nonetheless, she went on to lose in the December runoff election to Republican Bill Cassidy.

NOTE

1. "Key Capitol Hill Hearings," *C-SPAN*, 5 Nov 2014, https://archive.org/details/CSPAN
_20141105_070000_Key_Capitol_Hill_Hearings/start/2820/end/2880.

56

MIKE LEE

US Senator from Utah

Foundation on Christ

And now, my sons, remember, remember that it is upon the rock of our Redeemer, who is Christ, the Son of God, that ye must build your foundation; that when the devil shall send forth his mighty winds, yea, his shafts in the whirlwind, yea, when all his hail and his mighty storm shall beat upon you, it shall have no power over you to drag you down to the gulf of misery and endless wo, because of the rock upon which ye are built, which is a sure foundation, a foundation whereon if men build they cannot fall.

—Helaman 5:12 (Book of Mormon)

The senator from Utah grew up in a devout Mormon family, and his father, Rex Lee, was a president of The Church of Jesus Christ of Latter-day Saints' Brigham Young University. Senator Lee, an Eagle Scout and later student body president of BYU, also served two years as a Latter-day Saint missionary in McAllen, Texas.

"My faith informs everything I do," he said. "It certainly informs how I do my job, how I treat my family, and how I interact with others; so yes, it informs everything I do."

When asked what the essence of his faith was, Lee replied that Christ was his foundation. "It's following Jesus Christ, the redeemer of the world, the Son of God who took upon himself the sins of mankind and made it possible for us to receive forgiveness and to be resurrected after this life," he said.[1] This view is complemented by Lee's favorite scripture.

When asked by this author what his favorite verse was, Lee did not hesitate. "Helaman 5:12," he promptly replied. This is from the Book of Mormon, which Latter-day Saints consider "Another Testament of Jesus Christ" and a companion volume to the Old Testament and New Testament. In this chapter of the Book of Mormon, the ancient American soldier and prophet Helaman is giving advice to his sons, and he admonishes them to build their lives with Jesus Christ as their foundation (quoted above).[2] This is fatherly advice that Lee takes to heart, too.

NOTES

1. Adam Williams, "Senator Mike Lee on His Mormonism," *Mormon Hub,* 14 Jul 2014, https://mormonhub.com/blog/buzz/senator-mike-lee-mormonism.
2. Personal conversation with the author, 21 Feb 2017, Utah State Capitol.

57

JOE LIEBERMAN

US Senator from Connecticut

Rejuvenated by the Sabbath

Remember the day, Shabbat, to set it apart for God.

—Exodus 20:8 (Complete Jewish Bible)

H e was the first Jew on a major party's presidential ticket when Al Gore
tapped him to be his vice-presidential running mate in 2000, and he
later made waves leaving the Democratic Party to become an Independent.
His grandparents were Jewish immigrants from Poland and Austria-Hungary.
His wife, Hadassah, is the daughter of Holocaust survivors. Joe Lieberman is
also known as a passionate observer of the Sabbath and even wrote a book on
it, *The Gift of Rest: Rediscovering the Beauty of the Sabbath.*

The Liebermans attempt each weekend, from sunset on Fridays to sunset
on Saturdays, to follow the thirty-nine categories of rabbinical stipulations
for properly observing the Jewish Sabbath—from not riding in automo-
biles, to not cooking, engaging in business, or handling money. Instead,
they light candles, recite prayers, dine on simple meals, sing songs, or enjoy

what Lieberman has called one "of God's great blessings," the Sabbath afternoon nap.

"We aspire to work hard and be creative for six days, and rest on the seventh day, hopefully with some sense of satisfaction about what we've done on the other six," Lieberman said.[1]

Regarding the commandment to remember the Sabbath, outlined in Exodus 20:8, Lieberman notes that after the creation of the world, God, too, rested on the seventh day. He said, "We are told to 'remember' the Sabbath, to remember particularly that the world has a purposive Creator. We are not here by accident. We got here as a result of God's creation."

He points out that a few books later, the obligation to keep holy the Sabbath is given again. This "is in context of God's liberation of the Jewish people from Egypt," he said. "It is an affirmation that God not only created us, but that He continues to *care* about His creation and about human history: 'And remember that thou wast a servant in the land of Egypt, and that the Lord thy God brought thee out from there with a mighty hand and a stretched out arm: therefore the Lord thy God commanded thee to keep the Sabbath day'" (Deuteronomy 5:15, Third Millennium Bible).[2]

He said, "Observing the Sabbath is a commandment I have embraced, the fourth commandment to be exact, which Moses received from God on Mt. Sinai. Most of the time, it feels less like a commandment and more like a gift from God."

"For me, Sabbath observance is a gift because it is one of the deepest, purest pleasures in life," he said. To Lieberman, the Sabbath is filled "with beautiful settings, soaring melodies, wonderful food and wine, and lots of love. It's a time to reconnect with family and friends—and, of course, with God, the Creator of everything," he said. "Sabbath observance is a gift that has anchored, shaped, and inspired my life."

He notes that Christian and Jewish Americans alike used to be more diligent in observing the Sabbath, and yet a day of rest is needed today more than ever. "The Sabbath is an old but beautiful idea that, in our frantically harried and meaning-starved culture, cries out to be rediscovered and enjoyed by people of all faiths."

For him, the day of rest is almost transcendental. "In many ways, the Sabbath is an entirely different place from the one in which we live our weekday lives. It's a place away from clocks and watches, bound only by the natural movements of the sun," he said. "Entering the Sabbath is like stepping into a different world defined not by geographical boundaries but by faith, tradition, and spirituality."[3]

NOTES

1. Eric Marrapodi, "My Faith: Sen. Joe Lieberman embraces 'the gift of the Sabbath,'" *CNN*, 17 Aug 2011, http://religion.blogs.cnn.com/2011/08/17/my-faith-sen-joe-lieberman-embraces -the-gift-of-the-sabbath/.
2. Joe Lieberman, *The Gift of Rest: Rediscovering the Beauty of the Sabbath* (New York: Howard Books, 2011), 5–6.
3. Ibid., 3–4.

58

ABRAHAM LINCOLN

Sixteenth President of the United States

True and Righteous Judgments

Judge not, that ye be not judged. —*Matthew 7:1 (KJV)*

Woe unto the world because of offences! for it must needs be that offences come; but woe to that man by whom the offence cometh!

—*Matthew 18:7 (KJV)*

And I heard another out of the altar say, Even so, Lord God Almighty, true and righteous are thy judgments.

—*Revelation 16:7 (KJV)*

When Abraham Lincoln was sworn in as president for his second term, on March 4, 1865, he was very particular about having three verses marked in the Bible he was sworn in on. The three verses (shared above) are about judging others, offending others, and God's righteous judgments.[1]

Lincoln's second inaugural address has become known as "American Scripture." In just 703 words, he refers to "God" six times, the "Almighty" once, quotes the Bible directly three times, and alludes to scriptural verses several more times.

We know that Lincoln valued the verse from Matthew 7 because he wanted to be sworn in on it and because he paraphrased it in his speech. When talking about the slaveholders of the South, he said, "It may seem strange that any men should dare to ask a just God's assistance in wringing their bread from the sweat of other men's faces, but let us judge not, that we be not judged." This biblical attitude became the keystone for how Lincoln viewed the rebellious South, and the spirit of forgiveness in which he would have carried out Reconstruction.

Lincoln shared the verse from Matthew 18 in his address, too; then he added, "If we shall suppose that American slavery is one of those offenses which, in the providence of God, must needs come, but which, having continued through His appointed time, He now wills to remove, and that He gives to both North and South this terrible war as the woe due to those by whom the offense came, shall we discern therein any departure from those divine attributes which the believers in a living God always ascribe to Him?"

Finally, Lincoln put in context his beloved scripture from Revelations 16: "Fondly do we hope, fervently do we pray, that this mighty scourge of war may speedily pass away. Yet, if God wills that it continue until all the wealth piled by the bondsman's two hundred and fifty years of unrequited toil shall be sunk, and until every drop of blood drawn with the lash shall be paid by another drawn with the sword, as was said three thousand years ago, so still it must be said 'the judgments of the Lord are true and righteous altogether.'"[2]

Perhaps it is not surprising that one of Lincoln's finest and most enduring speeches so reverenced the will of God. Honest Abe had revered scripture his whole life. "I believe the Bible is the best gift God has ever given man. All the good from the Savior of the world is communicated to us through this book. But for it we could not know right from wrong," the revered Republican rail-splitter once said. "It is the duty of nations as well as men to recognize the truth announced in Holy Scripture and proven by all of history that those nations only are blessed whose God is the Lord."[3]

NOTES

1. Mahita Gajanan, "These Are the Bible Verses Past Presidents Have Turned to on Inauguration Day," *Time*, 19 Jan 2017, http://time.com/4639596/inauguration-day-presidents-bible-passages.

See also Ted Olsen, "Inaugural Scriptures," *Christian History,* 20 Jan 2009, http://www.christianitytoday.com/history/2009/january/inaugural-scriptures.html.

2. "Abraham Lincoln's second inaugural address." *Wikipedia,* retrieved 9 Apr 2017. See also Paul Edwards, "American Scripture: Lincoln's Second Inaugural Address," *God and Culture,* 15 Jan 2009, http://www.godandculture.com/blog/american-scripture-lincolns-second-inaugural-address.

3. Tim George, "American Presidents and the Bible," *Off the Grid News,* retrieved 21 Mar 2017, http://www.offthegridnews.com/misc/american-presidents-and-the-bible.

59

MIA LOVE

US Representative from Utah

Trusting in God through Unique Paths

*Behold, God is my salvation; I will trust, and not be afraid; for the Lord
Jehovah is my strength and my song; he also has become my salvation.*

—*2 Nephi 22:2 (Book of Mormon)*

B orn in New York City as the daughter of immigrants, joining The Church
of Jesus Christ of Latter-day Saints while in college in Connecticut, and
eventually serving as a mayor of a fast-growing Utah city, Mia Love made
history in 2014 when she was elected the first black female Republican to
Congress. "However anyone judges her politics, Love has expanded the
public image of what it means to be a black woman," wrote Mary C. Curtis
in the *Washington Post*. "Mia Love is black, Mormon, Republican and blowing people's minds."[1]

She was raised in the Roman Catholic faith of her parents and was intro-
duced to the Latter-day Saint faith by her sister Cyndi.[2] "My sister is Mormon
and I was invited to join her for a Church meeting," Love said. "I remember a
man talking from the pulpit, and he was encouraging the other men to 'love

their wife as Jesus loves the church.' He began to talk about eternal families and how everything that the church teaches us is to protect and nurture those relationships. I chose to follow this faith because if the man that I chose to marry someday was being taught those concepts, I would be grateful and happy." She later married Jason Love, a missionary she had met in Connecticut, and whom she described as "the greatest human being I know. I am happy."[3]

In the Book of Mormon, the ancient American prophet Nephi included in the record much of the Old Testament prophet Isaiah. "And now I write some of the words of Isaiah, that whoso of my people shall see these words may lift up their hearts and rejoice," he said (2 Nephi 11:8). When asked by this author what a favorite scripture was, Love indicated 2 Nephi 22:2, one of the Isaiah verses, similar to Isaiah 12:2.[4] "You're going to find a lot of similarities with any Christian faith," Love once said of her Mormonism.[5]

"Behold, God is my salvation; I will trust, and not be afraid; for the Lord Jehovah is my strength and my song; he also has become my salvation," says the verse. Navigating historic paths, Love says she has had to rely on God for strength and courage.

"As the only LDS woman in Congress, I know that I don't fit into many people's views of what a representative should look like," she said. "And as the child of immigrant parents from Haiti, I know how uncomfortable it can be to defy expectations. I frequently receive derogatory comments from people who have trouble accepting the fact that I don't fit in their small box. But I refuse to disappear in Congress just because I'm unique."[6]

NOTES

1. Mary C. Curtis, "Mia Love is black, Mormon, Republican and blowing people's minds," *Washington Post*, 12 Nov 2014, https://www.washingtonpost.com/blogs/she-the -people/wp/2014/11/12/mia-love-is-black-mormon-republican-and-blowing-peoples-minds /?noredirect=on&utm_term=.75d870817a28.

2. Matt Canham, "Mia Love: Searching for stardom; a Mormon conversion," *Deseret News*, 23 Dec 2014, https://www.sltrib.com/news/politics/2014/12/24/mia-love-searching-for-star dom-a-mormon-conversion.

3. Mia Love, "Hi I'm Mia. I'm a Mormon," *Mormon.org*, retrieved 8 Jun 2018, https://www .mormon.org/me/1n1q.

4. Personal text message with the author, 16 May 2018.

5. FoxNews.com, "Rising GOP star Mia Love glides into the spotlight at convention," *Fox News*, 28 Aug 2012, https://web.archive.org/web/20141105161139/http://www.foxnews.com /politics/2012/08/28/republican-convention-to-feature-rising-star-mia-love.

6. Mia Love, "Recognize that diversity gives us strength," *Deseret News*, 31 Mar 2018, https:// www.deseretnews.com/article/900014532/mia-love-recognize-that-diversity-gives-us-strength .html.

60

JAMES MADISON

Fourth President of the United States

Comfort in the Grace of God

Fear not, little flock; for it is your Father's good pleasure to give you the kingdom.

—Luke 12:32 (KJV)

The shortest president (five feet, four inches tall) was also known as the Father of the Constitution for his important work crafting that document in 1787. He was schooled as an Anglican, and he studied the Bible, theology, and Hebrew at Princeton.

James Madison was not very vocal about his personal religious views, but he would join his Quaker wife, Dolly, for occasional services at St. John's Episcopal Church near the White House. Throughout his life, Madison read books on theology for relaxation.[1]

In the margins of his Bible, Madison referenced Luke 12:32 specifically and wrote by it, "Grace, it is the free gift of God." Madison felt that belief in this merciful God was key to "the capacity of mankind for self-government."

In 1788 he wrote, "The belief in God all powerful wise and good, is so essential to the moral order of the world and to the happiness of man."[2]

NOTES

1. John C. McCollister, *God and the Oval Office* (Nashville: W Publishing Group, 2005), 23–25.
2. "One Nation Under God: America's Christian Heritage," *Christian Defense Fund*, retrieved 4 Apr 2017, http://www.leaderu.com/orgs/cdf/onug/madison.html.

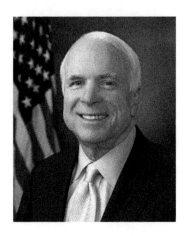

61

JOHN McCAIN

US Senator from Arizona

The Lord Is My Shepherd

Yea, though I walk through the valley of the shadow of death, I will fear
no evil: for thou art with me; thy rod and thy staff they comfort me.

—*Psalm 23:4 (KJV)*

John McCain was known for his long career in Congress, being the 2008
Republican presidential nominee, and for spending five and a half years as
a prisoner of war in Vietnam. His father and grandfather were both four-star
admirals, and he learned of faith by watching his dad. "My father didn't talk
about God or the importance of religious devotion. But, he did pray aloud
on his knees twice a day," McCain wrote.[1]

While a prisoner of war, McCain drew strength from his faith. For a
long time, the guards would torture the prisoners if they spoke aloud, so
"church" happened on Sunday afternoons after the midday meal, when the
dishes were washed and the guards had left. The senior officer would call
everyone to "church" by signaling the letter "c" with one cough followed
by three coughs. McCain and his fellow POWs would then silently say the

Pledge of Allegiance, recite the Lord's Prayer, and repeat Psalm 23: "The Lord is my shepherd; I shall not want . . ."

Later in the war, the North Vietnamese were less strict, and the POWs could have a simple Sunday service. McCain was asked to be the chaplain. "Not because the senior ranking officer thought I was imbued with any particular extra brand of religion, but because I knew all of the words of the Apostles' Creed and the Nicene Creed," he said.

"On Christmas Eve, the first time we had been together—some guys had been there as long as seven years—we had our service," McCain said. He had been given a Bible by a guard and had looked up the verses about the nativity to share. "We got to the point where we talked about the birth of Christ, and then sang 'Silent Night,' and I still remember looking at the faces of those guys—skinny, worn out—but most of them, a lot of them, had tears down their faces. And they weren't sorrow, they were happiness that for the first time in so many years we were able to worship together."[2]

Later as a senator, McCain still considered himself a man of faith. While he listed himself as an Episcopalian in official congressional biographies, he has also attended the North Phoenix Baptist Church for a couple of decades. While his wife, Cindy, was baptized there, McCain never was.[3]

When asked by the *New York Times* if he considered himself an evangelical Christian, he answered, "I consider myself a Christian. I attend church; my faith has sustained me in very difficult times," he said. "But I think it depends on what you call a quote evangelical Christian. Because there are some people who may not share my views on—I mean, that covers a lot of ground. But I certainly consider myself a Christian."[4]

NOTES

1. "McCain Blames Recession on Wall St.," *CBS News,* 21 Sep 2008, https://www.cbsnews.com/news/mccain-blames-recession-on-wall-st/6/.
2. Linda Feldmann, "John McCain: keeping faith, on his own terms," *Christian Science Monitor,* 18 Oct 2007, https://www.csmonitor.com/2007/1018/p01s06-uspo.html.
3. Manya A. Brachear, "John the Baptist? Ask voters," *Chicago Tribune,* 31 Aug 2008, http://www.chicagotribune.com/news/opinion/chi-mccain-perspectaug31-story.html.
4. "The Times Interviews John McCain," *New York Times,* 13 Jul 2008, http://www.nytimes.com/2008/07/13/us/politics/13text-mccain.html?_r=2&sq=John%20McCain&st=nyt&scp=4&pagewanted=print&oref=slogin&oref=slogin.

62

MITCH MCCONNELL

US Senate Majority Leader

Comfort in the Word

For now we see through a glass, darkly; but then face to face: now I know
in part; but then shall I know even as also I am known.

—*1 Corinthians 13:12 (KJV)*

Mitch McConnell is the longest-serving senator from Kentucky in history, the fifteenth Republican to lead his party in the Senate, and a lifelong Baptist. For a long time, McConnell was a member of the Crescent Hill Baptist Church in Louisville, but today he identifies with an evangelical megachurch associated with the Independent Christian Churches / Churches of Christ called the Southeast Christian Church.[1]

McConnell finds comfort in the words of the scriptures. For example, in remarks from the Senate floor following the shooting at Sandy Hook Elementary School in Newtown, Connecticut, McConnell shared some of the Bible verses he hoped would provide some comfort.

"Scripture says that while 'now we only know in part, in the life to come we shall know, even as we are known,'" he said, paraphrasing 1 Corinthians

13:12, about how someday we will understand why things happen the way they do.

He continued, quoting Revelation 21:4, "Scripture also says that in that day, 'every tear will be wiped away, because there will be no more death, or sorrow, or crying, or pain, for the former things will have passed away.'"

McConnell concluded, "May the people of Newtown and all Americans be consoled by this certain hope. May their burdens be lightened by the loving care of their neighbors and friends and even strangers in the days and weeks ahead. And may this terrible tragedy prompt all of us to cherish the lives we've been given, our family members and friends, and all who surround us in our daily tasks."[2]

NOTES

1. Aaron Douglas Weaver, "Baptists in Congress," *The Big Daddy Weave,* retrieved 7 Sep 2016, http://www.thebigdaddyweave.com/baptists-in-the-111th-congress.
2. "Minority Leader McConnell on Connecticut School Shootings," *C-SPAN,* 17 Dec 2012, https://www.c-span.org/video/?309976-6/minority-leader-mcconnell-connecticut-school-shootings.

63

MIKE MCINTYRE

US Representative from North Carolina

Biblical Inspiration

Where there is no vision, the people perish: but he that keepeth the law, happy is he.

—*Proverbs 29:18 (KJV)*

McIntyre represented the Tar Heel State in Congress for eighteen years but was also a lay leader in his hometown's First Presbyterian Church of Lumberton. There he served as an elder, deacon, Sunday School teacher, and chairman of the Weekday School and Day Care Committee.

He was pleased to speak on the floor of the House of Representatives during National Bible Week in 2007. "I'm grateful that we would take time tonight to celebrate not only the historical importance, but the personal importance that this great book, the best seller of all time, has for people literally the world over," the Democratic congressman said.

Of the Bible, he said, "The book is known as a book of encouragement, a book of enlightenment, and a book of edification." McIntyre shared some of his favorite verses in each of those areas, including a favorite proverb.

"As many of my friends back home in North Carolina know," he said, "my favorite Old Testament verse is from Proverbs 29:18, that says, 'Where there is no vision, the people perish.' And I think that's a great challenge to us, as leaders in this country, to have vision for where we want to take our country and what we want to do and how we want to solve the problems." He pointed out that this very verse is inscribed in the Science Committee room of the Rayburn House Office Building.

"The Bible allows us to see ourselves through its many stories and parables and prophecies and teachings," McIntyre concluded. "It also shows the flaws and frailties that we all share in common in humanity. It also shows the fellowship, both human and divine, that calls forth those values that so often we look for in our society today, values of forgiveness, of faithfulness and of fulfillment in becoming all that we know that we can become."[1]

NOTE

1. *Congressional Record*, 110th Congress, 1st Session, Issue: Vol. 153, No. 170, 5 Nov 2007, https://www.congress.gov/congressional-record/2007/11/05/house-section/article/H12483-4.

64

WILLIAM McKINLEY

Twenty-Fifth President of the United States

Yearning for Wisdom

Give me now wisdom and knowledge, that I may go out and come in before this people: for who can judge this thy people, that is so great?

—*2 Chronicles 1:10 (KJV)*

He that handleth a matter wisely shall find good: and whoso trusteth in the Lord, happy is he.
    The wise in heart shall be called prudent: and the sweetness of the lips increaseth learning.

—*Proverbs 16:20–21 (KJV)*

A lifelong Methodist, McKinley publicly embraced prayer, Christian kindness, and the Bible. "The more profoundly we study this Book and the more closely we observe its divine precepts," he said of the Bible, "the better citizens we will become and the higher will be our destiny as a nation."[1]

Surely McKinley had many favorite verses of the Bible, but as the president he gravitated toward those dealing with wisdom. For his first inaugural, he had a Bible, which was a gift from the bishops of the African Methodist Episcopal Church, opened to the prayer of King Solomon. Like the new king of Israel, the new president of the United States sought the gift of "wisdom and judgement."[2]

In 1899, McKinley was at the White House speaking to the General Missionary Committee of the Methodist Episcopal Church. The Republican from Ohio shared with them his divine inquiry into what to do with the weighty issue of his day—intervening in the Spanish-controlled Philippines during the Spanish-American War. "I walked the floor of the White House night after night until midnight, and I am not ashamed to tell you, gentlemen, that I went down on my knees and prayed to Almighty God for light and guidance more than one night." The answer then came to him clearly that America must help the Filipinos. "And by God's grace to do the very best we could by them," he said, "as our fellow-men for whom Christ also died. And then I went to bed, and went to sleep, and slept soundly."[3]

In his second inaugural, McKinley acknowledged that God had on many occasions shown him wisdom. He had the Bible opened to Proverbs 16:20–21, declaring the happiness of the wise who trust in the Lord.[4]

NOTES

1. Art Farstad, "The Bible and the Presidents," *Faith Alone Magazine,* retrieved 21 Mar 2017, https://faithalone.org/magazine/y1992/92feb1.html.
2. "The 28th Presidential Inauguration," Joint Congressional Committee on Inaugural Ceremonies, retrieved 11 Apr 2017, https://www.inaugural.senate.gov/about/past-inaugural-ceremonies/28th-inaugural-ceremonies.
3. "God in the White House," *PBS,* retrieved 4 Apr 2017, http://www.pbs.org/godinamerica/god-in-the-white-house.
4. "The 29th Presidential Inauguration," Joint Congressional Committee on Inaugural Ceremonies, retrieved 11 Apr 2017, https://www.inaugural.senate.gov/about/past-inaugural-ceremonies/29th-inaugural-ceremonies.

65

RICHARD M. NIXON

Thirty-Seventh President of the United States

Swords into Plowshares

And it shall come to pass in the last days, that the mountain of the Lord's house shall be established in the top of the mountains, and shall be exalted above the hills; and all nations shall flow unto it.

And many people shall go and say, Come ye, and let us go up to the mountain of the Lord, to the house of the God of Jacob; and he will teach us of his ways, and we will walk in his paths: for out of Zion shall go forth the law, and the word of the Lord from Jerusalem.

And he shall judge among the nations, and shall rebuke many people: and they shall beat their swords into plowshares, and their spears into pruninghooks: nation shall not lift up sword against nation, neither shall they learn war any more.

—Isaiah 2:2–4 (KJV)

R ichard Nixon worked hard in his roles as vice president, president, and senior statesmen to tame the geopolitical tigers of his day. He is remembered for being the only president to resign from office—but also for ending

American involvement in the Vietnam War, opening up Communist China, and working alongside Secretary of State Henry Kissinger to find stability and peace.

So perhaps it is not surprising that Nixon loved the words of Isaiah that spoke of turning swords into plowshares. In both his 1969 and 1973 inaugurations, he used two Bibles to be sworn in on. Both Bibles, both times, he had opened to Isaiah 2:2–4 (quoted above).[1]

In October 1969, Nixon made a statement about National Bible Week. "Throughout our history, despairing men and women have found sustaining solace in the word of God as written in the Bible," said Nixon, a Quaker. "Families have been guided by its enlightened precepts. Statesmen and leaders have drawn inspiration from its teachings, and courage from the enriching experience it records."

The Republican president from California continued, "It is unique among books and treasured by men and nations. And the power of the universal truths it holds is appropriately refreshed within our hearts on this occasion. The past has truly proved that we have much to gain by our devotion to the Scriptures. And the future holds great promise if we heed past lessons well."

In appreciation of his support, W. Clement Stone, the chairman of National Bible Week, presented Nixon with a miniature copy of a statue that represented the president's favorite verses. Entitled "We Shall Beat Our Swords into Plowshares," the original statue is at the United Nations Headquarters in New York.[2]

NOTES

1. "The 47th Presidential Inauguration," Joint Congressional Committee on Inaugural Ceremonies, retrieved 11 Apr 2017, https://www.inaugural.senate.gov/about/past-inaugural -ceremonies/47th-inaugural-ceremonies.
2. Richard Nixon, "Statement about National Bible Week," 22 Oct 1969, in Gerhard Peters and John T. Woolley, *The American Presidency Project*, http://www.presidency.ucsb.edu /ws/?pid=2279.

66

BARACK OBAMA

Forty-Fourth President of the United States

God Is Our Refuge and Strength

God is our refuge and strength, a very present help in trouble.

Therefore will not we fear, though the earth be removed, and though the mountains be carried into the midst of the sea;

Though the waters thereof roar and be troubled, though the mountains shake with the swelling thereof. Selah.

There is a river, the streams whereof shall make glad the city of God, the holy place of the tabernacles of the most High.

God is in the midst of her; she shall not be moved: God shall help her, and that right early.

The heathen raged, the kingdoms were moved: he uttered his voice, the earth melted.

The Lord of hosts is with us; the God of Jacob is our refuge. Selah.

Come, behold the works of the Lord, what desolations he hath made in the earth.

He maketh wars to cease unto the end of the earth; he breaketh the bow, and cutteth the spear in sunder; he burneth the chariot in the fire.

Be still, and know that I am God: I will be exalted among the heathen, I will be exalted in the earth.
The Lord of hosts is with us; the God of Jacob is our refuge. Selah.

—Psalm 46 (KJV)

In the New Hampshire Democratic debate in September 2007, then-Senator Barack Obama was asked, along with the others, "What is your favorite Bible verse?" He answered, "The Sermon on the Mount, because it expresses a basic principle that I think we've lost over the last six years."[1]

Obama referenced the Sermon on the Mount the following year again, in an October 2008 interview. "My Bible tells me there is nothing wrong with helping other people, that we want to treat others like we want to be treated," he said, "that I am my brother's keeper, and I am my sister's keeper. I believe that."[2]

A member of Chicago's Trinity United Church of Christ, Obama would reference the Bible plenty of times in his presidency. Although he was always sworn in on a closed Bible, Barack Obama quoted scripture in his first inaugural. "We remain a young Nation, but in the words of Scripture, the time has come to set aside childish things," he said, pointing to 1 Corinthians 13:11.[3]

In an interview with *Cathedral Age*, President Obama was asked if he had any favorite scriptural passages. "I do have a few favorites. Isaiah 40:31 has been a great source of encouragement in my life, and I quote from it often," he said. This is the verse that was also one of George W. Bush's favorites: "They shall mount up with wings as eagles."

"Psalm 46 is also important to me; I chose to read it on the tenth anniversary of 9/11," Obama added. This psalm is shared above. In fact, the entire psalm without any other commentary was the president's entire speech that day. "Niebuhr's serenity prayer is a good one as well," he said, referring to the prayer written by American theologian Reinhold Niebuhr:

God, grant me the serenity to accept the things I cannot change,
Courage to change the things I can,
And wisdom to know the difference.

"I've also been blessed to receive a daily devotional from my faith advisor, Joshua DuBois," he added, "who will send me Scripture or thoughts from people such as C. S. Lewis or Howard Thurman every morning."[4]

Notes

1. Jeff Zeleny, "The Democrats Quote Scripture," *New York Times*, 27 Sep 2007, https://thecaucus.blogs.nytimes.com/2007/09/27/the-democrats-quote-scripture/comment-page-3/?_r=1.
2. Barack Obama, "Barack Obama on Biblical Justification for Helping Others," *Berkley Center for Religion, Peace & World Affairs,* 30 Oct 2008, https://berkleycenter.georgetown.edu/quotes/barack-obama-on-biblical-justification-for-helping-others.
3. "The 56th Presidential Inauguration," Joint Congressional Committee on Inaugural Ceremonies, retrieved 11 Apr 2017, https://www.inaugural.senate.gov/about/past-inaugural-ceremonies/56th-inaugural-ceremonies.
4. "Faith in America," *Cathedral Age,* 23 Mar 2016, https://cathedral.org/cathedral-age/faith-in-america-2.

67

MICHELLE OBAMA

First Lady of the United States

Following Christ Daily

And he said to them all, If any man will come after me, let him deny himself, and take up his cross daily, and follow me.

—*Luke 9:23 (KJV)*

The nation's first African-American First Lady grew up in the South Side of Chicago and was raised United Methodist. She married Barack Obama in the Trinity United Church of Christ, and while in the White House, the Obamas attended Shiloh Baptist Church and St. John's Episcopal Church.

She was passionate about her husband's campaign of hope and change, speaking of his administration in biblical tones at times. "We have an amazing story to tell," she said in Nashville during the 2012 presidential reelection campaign. "This president has brought us out of the dark and into the light," she said—phraseology close enough to descriptions of Jesus in Matthew 4:16 that it raised some eyebrows among religious conservatives.[1]

In speaking to a conference of the African Methodist Episcopal church, she also pointed to the life of Jesus Christ as a model for daily persistence in citizenship and advocacy. "Our faith journey isn't just about showing up on Sunday for a good sermon and good music and a good meal," she said, emphasizing the daily living of one's religion as is admonished in Luke 9:23 (quoted above). "It's about what we do Monday through Saturday as well, especially in those quiet moments, when the spotlight's not on us, and we're making those daily choices about how to live our lives."

She continued, "We see that in the life of Jesus Christ. Jesus didn't limit his ministry to the four walls of the church," she said. "He was out there fighting injustice and speaking truth to power every single day. He was out there spreading a message of grace and redemption to the least, the last, and the lost. And our charge is to find Him everywhere, every day, by how we live our lives."[2]

NOTES

1. Daniel Halper, "Michelle Obama: 'This President Has Brought Us out of the Dark and into the Light,'" *Weekly Standard*, 17 Apr 2012, http://www.weeklystandard.com/michelle -obama-this-president-has-brought-us-out-of-the-dark-and-into-the-light/article/640374.
2. Devin Dwyer, "Michelle Obama Cites Jesus as Model for Citizenship," *ABC News*, 29 Jun 2012, http://abcnews.go.com/blogs/politics/2012/06/michelle-obama-cites-jesus-as-model-for -citizenship.

68

MARTIN O'MALLEY

Governor of Maryland

Seeing the Light of God

Just to be is a blessing. Just to live is holy.
Worship is a way of seeing the world in the light of God.
God is of no importance unless He is of supreme importance.
Man's sin is in his failure to live what he is. Being the master of the
earth, man forgets that he is the servant of God.
We are closer to God when we are asking questions than when we
think we have the answers.

—Writings of Abraham Heschel, Jewish theologian and philosopher

Martin O'Malley, past mayor of Baltimore, governor of Maryland, and Democratic presidential candidate, grew up in an Irish Catholic home. He attended Catholic schools, like Our Lady of Lourdes School in Bethesda and Gonzaga College High School, and he graduated from the Catholic University of America. He has been described as a "Pope Francis Democrat" and "a pray-every-morning, church-every-Sunday believer."[1]

Sometimes his faith comes through in his politics, like when he blasted a Christmas Refugee Roundup in 2015 on Twitter, saying it "sounds like something Donald Trump would concoct. Remember: Jesus was a refugee child who fled death gangs."[2]

He combines prayer with his reading. "In the morning, I generally take time to pray and sometimes that's at Mass; other times it's just at home," he once told the *Huffington Post*. "At home, I try to take twenty minutes—half hour, if I can—to read what I call 'good stuff.'" O'Malley defines the "good stuff" as the writings of inspiring authors, Christian poets, and theologians, like C. S. Lewis, John O'Donohue, Karl Rahner, Ignatius of Loyola, Thomas Merton, and Richard Rohr. He draws strength especially from the words of Jewish theologian and philosopher Abraham Heschel and has read everything he could by him.

"My sense is that we're on the verge of a new awareness of just how important the whole person is," he said. "I don't know that it's necessarily religious in the institutional sense, but it certainly has a spiritual dimension, without which life loses meaning."[3]

NOTES

1. Cathy Grossman, "5 faith facts about Martin O'Malley: 'A Pope Francis Democrat,'" *Washington Post*, 29 May 2015, https://www.washingtonpost.com/national/religion/5-faith -facts-about-martin-omalley-a-pope-francis-democrat/2015/05/29/b083447e-063f-11e5 -93f4-f24d4af7f97d_story.html?utm_term=.8b69fb0c59ed.
2. "In desperation, Martin O'Malley uses the Bible to bash Donald Trump and justify left-wing policies . . . ," *The Right Scoop*, 24 Dec 2015, http://therightscoop.com/in-desperation-martin -omalley-uses-the-bible-to-bash-donald-trump-and-justify-left-wing-policies/.
3. Scott Conroy, "How Martin O'Malley Begins His Day: Prayer, Solitude And Some Very Non-Political Reading," *Huffington Post*, 29 Mar 2015, http://www.huffingtonpost.com /2015/03/29/martin-omalley-prayer-solitude-sleep_n_6964716.html?utm_hp_ref=tw.

69

SARAH PALIN

Governor of Alaska

Grounded in God

For God hath not given us the spirit of fear; but of power, and of love, and of a sound mind.

—*2 Timothy 1:7 (KJV)*

Sarah Palin, the former governor of Alaska, made history as the first woman on a Republican presidential ticket when she was chosen to be John McCain's running mate in 2008. She counts herself as a "Bible-believing Christian" that attends "a non-denominational Bible church." She said, "I was baptized Catholic as a newborn and then my family started going to non-denominational churches throughout our life."[1]

Even though she was baptized a Roman Catholic as an infant, she was baptized again as a teenager, this time at the Pentecostal Assemblies of God church in Wasilla by founding pastor Paul Riley. Palin thanks Riley for "bringing her to Jesus." At the age of thirty-eight, she switched to Wasilla Bible Church, preferring the children's programs there for her family.[2]

Palin is unabashed about her belief in the Bible and in Jesus. "I'm not shy about talking about my faith, because for me my faith, my family, and my freedom as an American are the most important things in my life," she said.

"I always have that foundation of faith that I can stand strong on and hold on to, to get through challenges. My faith in Christ is really, at the end of the day, my be-all end-all."

She believes that it is natural for humans to seek the divine, and that "everyone is born with a God-shaped void in their soul, in their heart. I think that everybody is seeking something more, beyond what it is that we can see, hear, feel and touch today here on this earth."

Palin is not a stranger to public criticism, but she draws strength from God to get through and be resilient. "Some of my challenges just may be on the front page of the paper that day. What I remember, though, is that God somehow, someway can turn it around for good. A lot of people say, 'Why are you still standing? How are you still standing? Why are you coming back for more?'" She said it is then her chance to say, "You know what? God strengthens me through the challenges and allows me to stay very, very grounded because of my family and my kids, reminding me of what's important every day."

Palin draws strength from the Bible in dealing with daily challenges and especially loves "the Bible verse that says, 'God hasn't given us a spirit of fear, but a spirit of power and might and a sound mind.'"

"That scripture [2 Timothy 1:7] reminds me that we don't have to be afraid," Palin explained, "that God will be there for us as we call upon Him, because He has given us all those gifts of the Holy Spirit if we call out for them."[3]

NOTES

1. Jay Newton-Small, "Transcript: TIME's interview with Sarah Palin," *Time,* 29 Aug 2008, http://content.time.com/time/printout/0,8816,1837536,00.html.

2. Amanda Coyne, "A visit to Palin's church," *Newsweek,* 1 Sep 2008, http://www.newsweek.com/visit-palins-church-88811.

3. Janet Chismar, "Sarah Palin Draws Strength from Scripture," *Billy Graham Evangelical Association,* 24 Nov 2009, https://billygraham.org/story/sarah-palin-draws-strength-from-scripture.

70

RAND PAUL

US Senator from Kentucky

Peacemakers Not War-Makers

Blessed are the peacemakers, for they will be called children of God.

—Matthew 5:9 (NIV)

M y faith has never been easy for me," Rand Paul said at the 2012 Family Research Council's Values Voter Summit. "Never been easy to talk about and never been without obstacles." He struggled to understand "how tragedy could occur in a world that has purpose and design."

In an interview with Daystar, the Republican senator talked about his faith struggles as a young man. "As a teenager, I found that something was missing and decided that I would find that in Jesus." He was first born again at age fifteen, but he had to go through several times of being born again. "It's something that—I tell people it didn't always stick, either. I don't know if that's . . . blasphemy to say you have to be saved more than once, but I think sometimes it takes more than once for people."[1]

He once quoted Fyodor Dostoyevsky as summarizing his own faith journey: "I did not come to my hosanna through childlike faith but through a fiery furnace of doubt."[2]

Paul was baptized an Episcopalian; attended Baylor, a Baptist school; graduated from medical school at Duke, which was founded by Methodists and Quakers; and today is a member of the Presbyterian Church in Bowling Green, Kentucky. Paul's wife, Kelley, is a deacon in their church. "Rand and I are both Christians, and our faith is very important to us," she said.[3]

But Paul still struggles with his faith at times. "I am a Christian but not always a good one," he confessed to the Values Voters Summit. "I'm not completely free of doubts. I struggle to understand man's inhumanity to man. I struggle to understand the horrible tragedies that war inflicts on our young men and women."

Some of Paul's challenges with belief are a result of his experiences as a physician. "I'm also somebody who's in science and medicine, so it's not always been easy for me to say, well, gosh, how do I see God's hand in this horrible, horrible thing that I'm seeing, how do I see God's presence in something—you see small children dying from brain tumors and this and that," he said. "Religion and faith isn't always easy. But I always keep coming back."[4]

Because Paul is a believer and a lover of freedom, he has been an outspoken advocate of religious liberties. "The First Amendment says keep government out of religion. It doesn't say keep religion out of government," he once said.

He's concerned about religious liberties being curtailed not just at home but also abroad. "From Boston to Zanzibar, there is a worldwide war on Christianity," he said at the 2013 Value Voters Summit. "Across the globe, Christians are under attack, almost as if we lived in the Middle Ages or if we lived under early Pagan Roman rule," he said.[5]

Rand Paul was one of the strongest opponents to intervention in Iraq and Afghanistan. He has been touched by St. Augustine's "just war theory" and said, "I think part of Republicans' problems, and, frankly, to tell you the truth, some in the evangelical Christian movement, I think have appeared too eager for war."

He explained, "When I read the New Testament, I read about Jesus; I don't see him being involved in the wars of his days," Paul said. "In fact, people rebuked him for not being the king. They wanted somebody to stand up to the Romans. He stood up in a different sort of way, but he didn't organize coalitions and guerilla bands and arm them."

He continued, "Now I'm not saying that you shouldn't have people who want to defend against evil, bad forces around the world, but I think you need to remember that [Jesus] was the Prince of Peace."

He points to the Sermon on the Mount in the scriptures. "We're talking about, 'Blessed are the peacemakers,'" he said of the teachings of Jesus, "not 'Blessed are the war-makers.'"[6]

NOTES

1. Sarah Pulliam Bailey, "Here's what we know about Sen. Rand Paul's faith: 'Never been easy,'" *Washington Post*, 7 Apr 2015, https://www.washingtonpost.com/news/acts-of-faith/wp/2015/04/07/heres-what-we-know-about-sen-rand-pauls-faith-never-been-easy/?utm_term=.1b6065c23dc4.
2. Ray Nothstine, "7 Interesting Facts about Rand Paul's Christian Faith," *Christian Post*, 27 May 2015, http://www.christianpost.com/news/hold-for-addition-5-interesting-facts-about-rand-pauls-christian-faith-139586/.
3. Bailey, "Here's what we know."
4. Ibid.
5. Nothstine, "7 Interesting Facts."
6. Napp Nazworth, "Rand Paul: Some Evangelicals 'Too Eager for War,'" *Christian Post*, 11 Apr 2013, http://www.christianpost.com/news/rand-paul-some-evangelicals-too-eager-for-war-93752.

71

NANCY PELOSI

Speaker of the US House of Representatives

Different Ways of Serving

There are many different gifts, but it is always the same Spirit;
There are many different ways of serving, but it is always the same
Lord.
There are many different forms of activity, but in everybody it is the
same God who is at work in them all.
The particular manifestation of the Spirit granted to each one is to
be used for the general good.

—*1 Corinthians 12:4–7 (NJB)*

Nancy Pelosi, America's first female Speaker of the House, grew up in an active family that was politically Democratic, ethnically Italian-American, and religiously Roman Catholic. She was raised going to Catholic schools, like Baltimore's Institute of Notre Dame for high school and Washington, DC's Trinity College.

While in the eighth grade, Pelosi had an audience at the Vatican with Pope Pius XII. Her father, a Maryland congressman, had arranged for the visit while the family was in Rome. "It was beyond anything you could ever imagine," she later recalled. "I remember the pope asked if I was in college, and I told my brother, 'The pope thinks I am in college,'" she said. Her brother laughed and informed her that "in Italy, college meant high school."

As a devout Catholic, Pelosi made an effort to greet other popes as well. In 1965, she was among the throngs lining the streets of Manhattan to cheer Pope Paul VI, the first visit of a sitting pope to the Western Hemisphere. She welcomed Pope John Paul II to California in the 1980s, kissed the ring of Pope Benedict XVI in 2008, and was part of the American delegation to see Pope Francis installed. "I love Benedict's writing and his speeches," she said, especially "God is love."[1]

She spoke of God's love at a National Prayer Breakfast in 2016, quoting both the Bible and the Qur'an about loving one's neighbor. "We know that this message, this command of love, is not confined to the New Testament," she said in an ecumenical way. "The same message stands at the center of the Torah and the teachings of the Prophet Mohammad too." She then read from the Qur'an: "None of you has faith until he loves for his brother or his neighbor what he loves for himself."[2]

Many of Pelosi's opponents have accused her of not being a true Catholic because of her pro-choice stance on abortion and support for gay rights. A writer at *Catholic Online* claimed that she is engaging in "obstinate denial of truths which must be believed by every Catholic Christian."[3] Pelosi responded, "I actually agree with the pope on more issues than many Catholics who agree with him on one issue."[4]

Perhaps it is not surprising, then, that at a bipartisan prayer service on the opening day of Congress in 2011 she shared 1 Corinthians 12:4–7 (quoted above). These verses point out that everyone has unique ways of serving and different forms of activity, but we all have the same God. "There are different kinds of service, but the same Lord," she said to the distinguished gathering in Washington's St. Peter's Catholic Church.[5]

One verse quoted by Pelosi has puzzled some: "The Bible tells us in the Old Testament, 'To minister to the needs of God's creation is an act of worship. To ignore those needs is to dishonor the God who made us,'" she said in a press release commemorating Earth Day 2008. "On this Earth Day, and every day, let us honor the earth and our future generations with a commitment to fight climate change," she said.[6] She loves this verse, and has quoted it at least nine times, including in speeches on the House floor and in official statements celebrating other holidays, like Christmas and Martin

Luther King Jr. Day.[7] However, it has raised eyebrows because nobody can find where in the Bible such a verse is from.

"It's not in the Bible," said Claude Mariottini, a professor of Old Testament at Northern Baptist Theological Seminary. "There is nothing that even approximates that."

"[It's] not one that I recognize," said John J. Collins, the Holmes professor of Old Testament criticism and interpretation at Yale Divinity School. "I assume that she means this is a paraphrase. But it wouldn't be a close paraphrase to anything I know of."

Pelosi's office later clarified that she was indeed paraphrasing and that she heard a priest give a sermon in the early 1990s who quoted this passage, saying it was from the Book of Isaiah in the Old Testament. Regardless of if it is an actual Bible verse or not, it is a statement that Pelosi deeply believes in.[8]

NOTES

1. Jennifer Steinhauer, "In Pelosi, Strong Catholic Faith and Abortion Rights Coexist," *New York Times*, 21 Sep 2015, https://www.nytimes.com/2015/09/22/us/politics/in-pelosi-strong-catholic-faith-and-abortion-rights-coexist.html.
2. Charlie Spiering, "Nancy Pelosi quotes Mohammed at National Prayer Breakfast," *Breitbart*, 4 Feb 2016, http://www.breitbart.com/big-government/2016/02/04/nancy-pelosi-quotes-prophet-mohammad-at-national-prayer-breakfast/.
3. Keith Fournier, "Nancy Pelosi, Boasting of her Devout Catholic faith, is a Heretic," *Catholic Online*, 17 Jul 2016, http://www.catholic.org/news/politics/story.php?id=69781.
4. Steinhauer, "In Pelosi, Strong Catholic Faith."
5. Liz Halloran, "Bipartisanship on the Hill? Living on a Prayer," *WBUR News*, 5 Jan 2011, http://www.wbur.org/npr/132678353/bipartisanship-on-the-hill-living-on-a-prayer.
6. Anne Schroeder Mullins, "Pelosi, chapter and verse?" *Politico*, 24 Apr 2008, http://www.politico.com/blogs/anneschroeder/0408/Pelosi_verse_for_verse.html.
7. Jim Hoft, "Pelosi Quotes Phony Bible Verse to Honor Goddess Earth," *Gateway Pundit*, 24 Apr 2008, http://www.thegatewaypundit.com/2008/04/pelosi-quotes-phony-bible-verse-to-honor-goddess-earth/.
8. Mullins, "Pelosi, chapter and verse?"

72

MIKE PENCE

Vice President of the United States

Wisdom from God

For I know the plans I have for you, declares the Lord, plans to prosper you and not to harm you, plans to give you hope and a future.

—*Jeremiah 29:11 (NIV)*

I'm a Christian, a conservative, and a Republican, in that order," Mike Pence is fond of saying. He is a devout believer, raised a Catholic, who became a born-again evangelical Catholic in college. "I gave my life to Jesus Christ, and that changed everything," Pence said. He is known for having daily scripture study with his family and regular prayer and church attendance. "My Christian faith is at the very heart of who I am," he said.[1]

"You know, over the mantle of our home, for nearly twenty years, has been a Bible verse that speaks of a promise our little family has claimed and Americans have cherished through the generations," Pence said. The verse is Jeremiah 29:11 (quoted above), and speaks of the plans God has for one's future.[2] The plans for Mike Pence included service as a member of Congress, governor of Indiana, and then vice president of the United States.

While accepting the Republican nomination for vice president in Cleveland, he quoted Solomon's plea for wisdom found in 2 Chronicles 1:10. "Should I have the awesome privilege to serve as your vice president," he declared, "I promise to keep faith with that conviction, to pray daily for a wise and 'discerning heart . . . for who is able to govern this great people of yours, O God?'"[3]

Mike Pence isn't afraid to reference verses of the Bible in explaining his political beliefs. "For me, the sanctity of life proceeds out of the . . . ancient principle where God says, 'Before you were formed in the womb, I knew you,'" he said on another occasion in explaining his view of abortion, referencing Jeremiah 1:5. "The very idea that a child almost born into the world could still have his life taken from him is just anathema to me."[4]

When it came time to be inaugurated as vice president, Pence chose to be sworn in on Ronald Reagan's family Bible, which had been transported from the Reagan Library for the occasion. He also chose to have the Bible opened to the same verse that Reagan had opened on both of his inaugurations, 2 Chronicles 7:14. This is part of the Lord's words to Solomon, saying that if people call on God's name, He "will forgive their sin and will heal their land."

Pence created this spiritual touchstone to Ronald Reagan as an auspicious way to begin his vice presidency. "President Ronald Reagan placed his faith in a loving God and the goodness of our country," he explained. "He set out to change a nation and in doing so, he changed the world."[5]

NOTES

1. Max Perry Mueller, "The Christian Worldview of Mike Pence," *Religion and Politics,* 10 Oct 2016, http://religionandpolitics.org/2016/10/10/the-christian-worldview-of-mike-pence.
2. Mike Pence, "Remarks by Vice President Pence at National Day of Prayer," *WhiteHouse.gov,* 3 May 2018, https://www.whitehouse.gov/briefings-statements/remarks-vice-president-pence -national-day-prayer.
3. Ken Klukowski, "Gov. Mike Pence's RNC Speech Included Bible Code Words to Christians," *Breitbart,* 23 Jul 2016, http://www.breitbart.com/2016-presidential-race/2016/07/23/gov -mike-pences-rnc-speech-included-bible-code-words-to-christians.
4. Ismat Sarah Mangla, "Tim Kaine and Mike Pence both used the Bible to say opposite things," *Quartz Media,* 5 Oct 2016, https://qz.com/800848/vice-presidential-debate-tim-kaine-and -mike-pence-both-used-the-bible-to-say-opposite-things.
5. "Trump being sworn in with 2 Bibles: His mother's and Abraham Lincoln's," *Fox8 Cleveland,* 20 Jan 2017, http://fox8.com/2017/01/20/trump-being-sworn-in-with-2-bibles-his-mothers -and-abraham-lincolns.

73

RICK PERRY

US Secretary of Energy

God Is with You

Have I not commanded you? Be strong and courageous. Do not be afraid; do not be discouraged, for the Lord your God will be with you wherever you go.

—*Joshua 1:9 (NIV)*

After George W. Bush resigned the Texas governorship to go to the White House, his lieutenant governor, Rick Perry, became governor of the Lone Star State. After over fourteen years in that post, he was appointed by President Donald Trump to be his Secretary of Energy.

Perry grew up enjoying the "comfort in tradition and stability" he found in a structured Methodist Church. "We sang the doxology, the preacher would preach, we would have a hymn," he said. The Perry family was long a member of Tarrytown United Methodist Church, a respected mainline protestant denomination.

But when the Governor's Mansion was under repair and he and his wife lived in a rental home, they became attracted to a nearby megachurch, Lake

Hills Church. The large, non-denominational evangelical church worships in a stadium-like sanctuary with rock bands and huge crowds. "They dunk," Perry said of another difference. "Methodists sprinkle."[1]

His views came out on the campaign trail. In 2006, he stirred up some controversy when he agreed with a minister who said those who don't accept Jesus as their savior will be condemned to hell. "In my faith, that's what it says, and I'm a believer of that," he said.

Later, Perry clarified, "I don't know that there's any human being that has the ability to interpret what God and his final decision-making is going to be." The Republican governor continued, "That's what the faith says. I understand, and my caveat there is that an all-knowing God certainly transcends my personal ability to make that judgment black and white."

He concluded: "Before we get into Buddha and all the others, I get a little confused there. But the fact is that we live in a pluralistic world but our faith is real personal. And my Christian faith teaches that the way is through Jesus Christ." Perry also noted that he believed in biblical inerrancy—that the Bible is without error or fault.[2]

Twice a candidate for president, Perry was once asked on the campaign trail what his favorite scripture was. "Right now it's Joshua 1:9," he said, "where He commanded us to be brave, be courageous, and not be afraid, because he will always be with us. And as we go through this process, and you look around, and every now and then you look behind in the parade you thought you were leading, and it might have thinned out a little bit. That's okay, because the one person you need to have in the parade with you is always there."[3]

NOTES

1. Joshunda Sanders and Jason Embry, "Candidates mirror population in attending more than one church," *Austin American-Statesman,* retrieved 25 Aug 2017, https://web.archive.org/web /20101106024905/http://www.statesman.com:80/news/texas-politics/governors_race/candi dates-mirror-population-in-attending-more-than-one-1009306.html.
2. Christy Hoppe, "Perry believes non-Christians doomed," *Dallas Morning News,* 6 Nov 2006, https://web.archive.org/web/20061119030904/http://www.dallasnews.com/sharedcontent /dws/dn/latestnews/stories/110606dnTSWperry.351c57c.html.
3. "Politics Public Policy Today," *CSPAN,* 17 Jan 2012, 5:02 am, https://archive.org/details /CSPAN_20120117_060000_Politics__Public_Policy_Today/start/14566/end/14626?q=% 22favorite+scripture%22.

74

CHARLIE RANGEL

US Representative from New York

Spiritual Things

For I was hungry and you gave me nothing to eat, I was thirsty and you gave me nothing to drink, I was a stranger and you did not invite me in, I needed clothes and you did not clothe me, I was sick and in prison and you did not look after me.

—Matthew 25:42–43 (NIV)

Everyone in Washington came to know the congenial, candid, and humorous Charlie Rangel, one of the longest serving members of Congress. Originally from Harlem and raised a Roman Catholic, Rangel was never afraid to call it how he saw it, including when he felt there was a religious and moral angle to the work being done in Congress.

In the 2011 fight to raise the debt ceiling so that Medicaid, Medicare, Social Security, and more could be funded, the Democratic congressman called on his colleagues to do "the Lord's work" and take care of the poor. "These are not political questions," he said. "These are moral questions." Looking at reporters, he said in his raspy voice, "Why don't you call your pastor, your rabbi, your imam? There has to be a moral answer." He asked his colleagues, "What would Jesus do?"[1]

Later, in a 2014 speech to labor union members, Rangel said, "The things we believe in are spiritual d--- things. You can talk about the union organizing and raising the minimum wage and extensive unemployment compensation, but isn't that the same thing as talking about someone that's hungry, that's thirsty, that's naked, that's in prison."

He continued, "Now I don't know where the h--- the spiritual leaders are going to be, but I haven't heard their voices when it comes to shelter. That has to be a part of [Matthew 25] in terms of how do you treat the less of my brothers and sisters."

"I haven't heard the church on homelessness, but I have to believe that God didn't intend for some people to live in luxury and other people to live in squalor," he said.[2]

NOTES

1. Bree Tracey, "Religion, Rangel and the Debt Ceiling," *Fox News,* 8 Jul 2011, http://www .foxnews.com/politics/2011/07/08/religion-rangel-and-debt-ceiling.html.
2. Craig Millward, "Charlie Rangel: 'The Things We Believe in Are Spiritual Damn Things,'" *CNS News,* 27 Oct 2014, http://www.cnsnews.com/news/article/craig-millward/charlie -rangel-things-we-believe-are-spiritual-damn-things.

75

RONALD REAGAN

Fortieth President of the United States

Seek His Face

If my people, which are called by my name, shall humble themselves, and pray, and seek my face, and turn from their wicked ways; then will I hear from heaven, and will forgive their sin, and will heal their land.

—*2 Chronicles 7:14 (KJV)*

Ronald Reagan believed in the Bible, and in the power of scripture to drive good civic behavior. "We might come closer to balancing the budget if all of us lived closer to the Commandments and the Golden Rule," he once quipped.[1]

When it came time for him to be sworn in as president, he used the family Bible he had inherited from his late mother, Nellie Reagan. He had it opened up to the words of God to King Solomon in 2 Chronicles 7:14.[2] This was a verse also loved by Eisenhower, and it was used in his first inauguration. But unlike his fellow two-term Republican predecessor, Reagan liked this verse so well that he used it for both of his inaugurations.

Reagan sincerely believed that the United States must seek God's face and turn from their wicked ways. "Sometimes, it seems we've strayed from [our] noble beginning, from our conviction that standards of right and wrong do exist and must be lived up to," he said at the National Prayer Breakfast in 1982. "We expect Him to protect us in a crisis, but turn away from Him too often in our day-to-day living. I wonder if He isn't waiting for us to wake up."[3]

The words in Chronicles guided his view of America's relationship with God. "I believe with all my heart that standing up for America means standing up for the God who has so blessed our land," he said on another occasion. "We need God's help to guide our nation through stormy seas. But we can't expect Him to protect America in a crisis if we just leave Him over on the shelf in our day-to-day living."

He continued, "America was founded by people who believe that God was their rock of safety. I recognize we must be cautious in claiming that God is on our side, but I think it's all right to keep asking if we're on His side."[4]

NOTES

1. "20 Ronald Reagan Quotes," *Christian Quotes,* retrieved 1 May 2017, https://www.chris tianquotes.info/quotes-by-author/ronald-reagan-quotes/#axzz4fsy1FW3o.

2. "The 50th Presidential Inauguration," Joint Congressional Committee on Inaugural Ceremonies, retrieved 11 Apr 2017, https://www.inaugural.senate.gov/about/past-inaugural -ceremonies/50th-inaugural-ceremonies/.

3. Ronald Reagan: "Remarks at the Annual National Prayer Breakfast," 4 Feb 1982, in Gerhard Peters and John T. Woolley, *The American Presidency Project.* http://www.presidency.ucsb .edu/ws/?pid=43075.

4. "20 Ronald Reagan Quotes," *Christian Quotes.*

76

HARRY REID

US Senate Majority Leader

Adversity Shall Be for Thy Good

And if thou shouldst be cast into the pit, or into the hands of murderers, and the sentence of death passed upon thee; if thou be cast into the deep; if the billowing surge conspire against thee; if fierce winds become thine enemy; if the heavens gather blackness, and all the elements combine to hedge up the way; and above all, if the very jaws of hell shall gape open the mouth wide after thee, know thou, my son, that all these things shall give thee experience, and shall be for thy good.

The Son of Man hath descended below them all. Art thou greater than he?

Therefore, hold on thy way, and the priesthood shall remain with thee; for their bounds are set, they cannot pass. Thy days are known, and thy years shall not be numbered less; therefore, fear not what man can do, for God shall be with you forever and ever.

—Doctrine and Covenants 122:7–9

Harry Reid grew up agnostic in the tiny Nevada town of Searchlight and joined The Church of Jesus Christ of Latter-day Saints while attending Utah State University. Rising from a city attorney to become a state legislator, the lieutenant governor of Nevada, a US Senator, and then the Senate Majority Leader, Reid was the highest-ranking elected official in Latter-day Saint history.

He was not shy about sharing his faith, and he always kept copies of the Book of Mormon in his Senate office. He gave them away to others who seemed in need of spiritual guidance. "A couple of years ago, I decided to give one to [Larry Pressler of South Dakota] a Republican senator whom I had served with for eighteen years," said Reid, a Democrat, in a *Salt Lake Tribune* interview. "He was no longer in the US Senate and his politics were different from mine, but we were friends."

Reid told him "Larry, here's the Book of Mormon. Read it. It may be good for you." Pressler did read the book, which is subtitled "Another Testament of Jesus Christ." Pressler ended up joining The Church of Jesus Christ of Latter-day Saints, and after his baptism Reid helped confirm him a member. "I'm not very pushy on my religion," he said. "I let other people do what they think is appropriate. But, at times, I felt it was the right thing to do, and it worked out well for Larry."

In that same interview, when asked what his favorite passage of scripture was, Reid did not select a scripture from the Book of Mormon or the Bible (which his faith also reveres as scripture). Instead, he chose one from the Doctrine and Covenants, a collection of divine revelations given to the Church founder, Joseph Smith, and some of his successors.

"Doctrine & Covenants section 122 means a lot to me, especially the setting," Reid said. "Joseph Smith is in Liberty Jail [in Missouri] and had been there a long time. He's complaining, 'Why are you letting these people do this to me?' He's told 'Because it's good for you.'"[1] For someone who has been through the rough and tumble of politics like Harry Reid, such words would indeed inspire comfort.

NOTE

1. Peggy Fletcher Stack, "Reid: No group is harder on me than fellow Mormons," *Salt Lake Tribune*, 21 Jan 2017, http://www.sltrib.com/home/4846862-155/former-sen-harry-reid-no -group.

77

MITT ROMNEY

US Senator from Utah

Compassionate Care to Others

*For I was an hungred, and ye gave me meat: I was thirsty, and ye gave
me drink: I was a stranger, and ye took me in:*

    *Naked, and ye clothed me: I was sick, and ye visited me: I was in
prison, and ye came unto me.*

—*Matthew 25:35–36 (KJV)*

M itt Romney, the former 2002 Salt Lake Winter Olympics CEO,
Massachusetts governor, and 2012 Republican presidential nominee,
has a deep heritage and background of faith as a member of The Church
of Jesus Christ of Latter-day Saints. Like his father, grandfather, and great-
grandfather, he had taken his turn proclaiming the gospel as a full-time missionary. In his case, he spent two and a half years sharing the Latter-day Saint
faith in France.

    "I was taught in my home to honor God and love my neighbor," Romney
said of his upbringing. "My father was committed to Martin Luther King
Jr.'s cause of equality, and I saw my parents provide compassionate care to

others, in personal ways to people nearby and in leading national volunteer movements. My faith is grounded in the conviction that a consequence of our common humanity is our responsibility to one another—to our fellow Americans foremost, but also to every child of God."

In a religion with a lay ministry, Romney later served five years as bishop of his Latter-day Saint congregation in Belmont, Massachusetts. Then, from 1986 to 1994, he served as president over a dozen congregations and four thousand members in eastern Massachusetts. In these duties, he sometimes spent thirty hours a week ministering to struggling members, visiting the sick, helping immigrants, and preparing sermons.

"Faith is integral to my life. I have served as a lay pastor in my church. I faithfully follow its precepts," he said. "I am often asked about my faith and my beliefs about Jesus Christ. I believe that Jesus Christ is the Son of God and the Savior of mankind."

When asked by *Cathedral Age,* the publication of Washington National Cathedral, what his favorite scripture was, Romney replied, "I am always moved by the Lord's words in Matthew: 'For I was an hungred, and ye gave me meat: I was thirsty, and ye gave me drink: I was a stranger, and ye took me in: Naked, and ye clothed me.'"[1]

While campaigning for president, Romney noted Bible passages on occasion but rarely made Latter-day Saint references or invoked the Book of Mormon in public. He did, however, paraphrase some Book of Mormon scripture in a statement after a shooting at a movie theater in a Denver suburb.

"Today we feel not only a sense of grief, but perhaps also of helplessness," Romney said. "But there is something we can do. We can offer comfort to someone near us who is suffering or heavy-laden. And we can mourn with those who mourn in Colorado."[2]

Romney's words hearken to the Book of Mormon's Mosiah 18:8–9: "As ye are desirous to come into the fold of God, and to be called his people, and are willing to bear one another's burdens, that they may be light; Yea, and are willing to mourn with those that mourn; yea, and comfort those that stand in need of comfort, and to stand as witnesses of God at all times and in all things, and in all places that ye may be in, even until death, that ye may be redeemed of God, and be numbered with those of the first resurrection, that ye may have eternal life."

NOTES

1. "Faith in America," *Cathedral Age,* 23 Mar 2016, https://cathedral.org/cathedral-age/faith -in-america-2/.
2. Peggy Fletcher Stack, "Romney quotes Book of Mormon in speech," *Salt Lake Tribune,* 20 Jul 2012, http://archive.sltrib.com/story.php?ref=/sltrib/blogsfaithblog/54528521-180 /mourn-romney-book-comfort.html.csp.

78

FRANKLIN D. ROOSEVELT

Thirty-Second President of the United States

Faith, Hope, and Charity

Though I speak with the tongues of men and of angels, and have not charity, I am become as sounding brass, or a tinkling cymbal.

And though I have the gift of prophecy, and understand all mysteries, and all knowledge; and though I have all faith, so that I could remove mountains, and have not charity, I am nothing.

And though I bestow all my goods to feed the poor, and though I give my body to be burned, and have not charity, it profiteth me nothing.

Charity suffereth long, and is kind; charity envieth not; charity vaunteth not itself, is not puffed up,

Doth not behave itself unseemly, seeketh not her own, is not easily provoked, thinketh no evil;

Rejoiceth not in iniquity, but rejoiceth in the truth;

Beareth all things, believeth all things, hopeth all things, endureth all things.

Charity never faileth: but whether there be prophecies, they shall fail; whether there be tongues, they shall cease; whether there be knowledge, it shall vanish away. . . .

And now abideth faith, hope, charity, these three; but the greatest of these is charity.

—*1 Corinthians 13:1–8, 13 (KJV)*

N ot an active church-going Episcopalian—much to his wife's chagrin—Roosevelt did have a personal faith in prayer and scripture reading that gave him strength as he battled polio and the demands of public life.

"We cannot read the history of our rise and development as a nation without reckoning with the place the Bible has occupied in shaping the advances of the Republic," he once said in tribute to the Good Book. "Where we have been truest and most consistent in obeying its precepts, we have attained the greatest measure of contentment and prosperity."[1]

On another occasion, Roosevelt expressed the value of biblical teachings. "I feel that a comprehensive study of the Bible is a liberal education for anyone," he said. "Nearly all of the great men of our country have been well-versed in the teachings of the Bible."[2]

FDR's knowledge of the Bible seeped through in his fireside chats to the nation. He loved to reference Psalm 23 ("The Lord is my shepherd"), the Beatitudes, and the thirteenth chapter of 1 Corinthians.

Roosevelt was especially influenced by 1 Corinthians 13, which was the chapter he wanted the Bible open to when he was sworn in not once, but each of the record four times he was inaugurated. The old Roosevelt family Bible was used each time, printed in Dutch in 1686 and therefore the oldest inaugural Bible ever used.[3]

So why was FDR so drawn to the chapter about faith, hope, and charity? He expounded on what he saw in those scriptural verses when accepting the Democratic nomination for reelection at his party's 1936 convention in Philadelphia:

> We do not see faith, hope, and charity as unattainable ideals, but we use them as stout supports of a Nation fighting the fight for freedom in a modern civilization.
>
> Faith—in the soundness of democracy in the midst of dictatorships.
>
> Hope—renewed because we know so well the progress we have made.
>
> Charity—in the true spirit of that grand old word. For charity literally translated from the original means love, the love that understands, that does not merely share the wealth of the giver, but in true sympathy and wisdom helps men to help themselves.

We seek not merely to make Government a mechanical implement, but to give it the vibrant personal character that is the very embodiment of human charity.

We are poor indeed if this Nation cannot afford to lift from every recess of American life the dread fear of the unemployed that they are not needed in the world. We cannot afford to accumulate a deficit in the books of human fortitude.

In the place of the palace of privilege we seek to build a temple out of faith and hope and charity.[4]

NOTES

1. Tim George, "American Presidents and the Bible," *Off the Grid News*, retrieved 21 Mar 2017, http://www.offthegridnews.com/misc/american-presidents-and-the-bible.
2. John C. McCollister, *God and the Oval Office* (Nashville: W Publishing Group, 2005), 158.
3. "The 37th Presidential Inauguration," Joint Congressional Committee on Inaugural Ceremonies, retrieved 11 Apr 2017, https://www.inaugural.senate.gov/about/past-inaugural-ceremonies/37th-inaugural-ceremonies.
4. "Franklin D. Roosevelt Acceptance Speech for the Renomination for the Presidency." *The American Presidency Project*, retrieved 15 Apr 2017, http://www.presidency.ucsb.edu/ws/?pid=15314.

79

THEODORE ROOSEVELT

Twenty-Sixth President of the United States

A Doer

But be ye doers of the word, and not hearers only, deceiving your own selves.

For if any be a hearer of the word, and not a doer, he is like unto a man beholding his natural face in a glass.

—*James 1:22–23 (KJV)*

He hath shewed thee, O man, what is good; and what doth the Lord require of thee, but to do justly, and to love mercy, and to walk humbly with thy God?

—*Micah 6:8 (KJV)*

Theodore Roosevelt was a force of nature. Living life with gusto, he boisterously advocated for the "strenuous life" and was a mover and shaker unlike anything the country had ever seen. This man of action was the youngest American president, being sworn in at age forty-two upon the death of William McKinley. After an energetic term as president, he was sworn in for a second term on March 4, 1905.

It surprised nobody that this man of action grabbed the same Bible he used when he was sworn in as governor of New York in 1898 and opened it to James 1:22–23 to be sworn in on as president for a second time.[1] "I believe in the gospel of works as put down in the Epistle of James," he once declared. "'Be ye doers of the word, and not hearers only.'" Roosevelt also loved James 2:20, "Faith without works is dead."[2]

The famous Rough Rider had a zeal for about everything in life, including the Bible. "Almost every man who by his life-work added to the sum of human achievement of which the race is proud, of which our people are proud," he once trumpeted, "almost every such man has based his life-work largely upon the teachings of the Bible."[3] On another occasion, this gregarious member of the Dutch Reformed Church declared, "A thorough knowledge of the Bible is worth more than a college education."[4]

His religion was the "muscular Christianity," and when nominated again for president in 1912 (this time by the Progressive Party), he rallied the faithful in his acceptance: "We stand at Armageddon and we battle for the Lord!" He then proceeded to lead the raptured crowd in singing "Onward, Christian Soldiers."[5]

Roosevelt's favorite hymns included "How Firm a Foundation" and "A Mighty Fortress Is Our God." In addition to the well-loved verses in James that he was sworn in on, it was also reported that his favorite verse of scripture was Micah 6:8, where we are told "to do justly, and to love mercy, and to walk humbly."[6]

NOTES

1. "The 30th Presidential Inauguration," Joint Congressional Committee on Inaugural Ceremonies, retrieved 11 Apr 2017, https://www.inaugural.senate.gov/about/past-inaugural-ceremonies/30th-inaugural-ceremonies.
2. John C. McCollister, *God and the Oval Office* (Nashville: W Publishing Group, 2005), 130.
3. Art Farstad, "The Bible and the Presidents," *Faith Alone Magazine*, retrieved 21 Mar 2017, https://faithalone.org/magazine/y1992/92feb1.html.
4. Debbie McDaniel, "31 Quotes and Verses: Reminders of Where Freedom Is Found," *Crosswalk.com*, 17 Feb 2017, http://www.crosswalk.com/faith/spiritual-life/inspiring-quotes/23-great-presidential-quotes-to-remind-us-of-what-keeps-america-free.html.
5. Rick Marschall, "A True Christian American President," *Christian Broadcasting Network*, retrieved 12 Apr 2017, http://www1.cbn.com/churchandministry/a-true-christian-american-president.
6. McCollister, *God and the Oval Office*, 128, 130. See also Marschall, "A True Christian American President."

80

MARCO RUBIO

US Senator from Florida

God's Guiding Path

Yours, O Lord, is the greatness and the power and the glory and the victory and the majesty, indeed everything that is in the heavens and the earth; Yours is the dominion, O Lord, and You exalt Yourself as head over all.

Both riches and honor come from You, and You rule over all, and in Your hand is power and might; and it lies in Your hand to make great and to strengthen everyone.

—1 Chronicles 29:11–12 (NASB)

Few of America's modern leaders have had the circuitous faith journey that the senator from Florida and one-time Republican presidential candidate Marco Rubio has had. A Cuban-American, Rubio was born into a traditional Catholic family, and when he was a young boy, on Sunday afternoons he would wrap himself in a sheet to "play priest" and mimic the service.

But while living near Latter-day Saint relatives in Nevada, Rubio and his family joined The Church of Jesus Christ of Latter-day Saints. "I immersed myself in LDS theology," Rubio wrote of the time when he was baptized, "and understood it as well as an eight-year-old mind can."[1]

However, his dad never converted, struggling as a bartender with the Mormon prohibition on alcohol. "We had extended family members who were and remain active members of the LDS church, which does provide a very wholesome environment," Rubio said. "We joined the church for a little less than three years," and then they went back to Catholicism.[2] He was married in the Church of the Little Flower, a Catholic church in Coral Gables, Florida.

As an adult, Rubio was impressed by a Southern Baptist Convention–affiliated evangelical megachurch that his wife and sister led him to, Christ Fellowship. "It does a phenomenal job on two fronts: bringing people to Jesus, and teaching the written Word through phenomenal preachers," said Rubio. And although four years later he "felt called back to Catholicism," he is still influenced by Christ Fellowship, listens to their podcasts, donates to them, and attends on occasion. "There has never been a moment when faith hasn't been an important part of my life," he said.[3]

The result of his journey was a deeper appreciation for the scriptures, and his faith was shaped by it. "I think too many Catholics don't fully understand their faith, and the result is I didn't learn about the Catholic Church until I went to a non-Catholic church," he said, "and became infused in the Bible and became infused in the written word of God, and then and only then did the liturgy of the church start even making sense. I started to begin to understand the richness of the church."[4]

Because of this understanding of the Bible, Rubio has a fluid and easy way of inserting verses into his political dialogue. Luke 12:48 was invoked in his speech at the 2012 Republican National Convention: "We're special because we've always understood the scriptural admonition, that for everyone to whom much is given, from him much is required," he said.[5]

When he launched his quest for the 2016 Republican presidential nomination, he quoted Joshua 1:9 in his kick-off speech. "In this endeavor, as in all things," he said, "I find comfort in the ancient command to 'be strong and courageous! Do not tremble or be dismayed, for the Lord your God is with you wherever you go.'"[6]

And when his race for the nomination came to an end, Rubio again shared scripture. "While it is not God's plan that I be president in 2016 or maybe ever," he said to supporters, "He has a plan for every one of our lives. Everything that comes from God is good. God is perfect. God makes no mistakes. And He has things planned for all of us." Rubio then quoted King

David in 1 Chronicles 29:11–12 (quoted above), a verse that captures his view that God is in his life and is guiding him through the ups and downs.[7]

NOTES

1. Michael Kruse, "Marco Rubio's Crisis of Faith," *Politico*, 22 Jan 2016, http://www.politico.com/magazine/story/2016/01/marco-rubios-crisis-of-faith-213553.
2. Sarah Pulliam Bailey, "Q & A: Marco Rubio on His Faith of Many Colors," *Christianity Today*, 19 Jun 2012, http://www.christianitytoday.com/ct/2012/july-august/marco-rubio-faith-of-many-colors.html.
3. Ibid.
4. Kruse, "Marco Rubio's Crisis of Faith."
5. James K. Aitken, Jeremy M. S. Clines, and Christl M. Maier, eds., *Interested Readers: Essays on the Hebrew Bible in Honor of David J. A. Clines* (Atlanta: Society of Biblical Literature, 2013), 210.
6. Barton Swaim, "The pitfalls of politicians citing Bible verses," *Washington Post*, 2 Dec 2015, https://www.washingtonpost.com/news/the-fix/wp/2015/12/02/if-a-2016-candidate-is-citing-a-bible-verse-theres-a-good-chance-its-not-quite-right/?utm_term=.f0f4aa8903e7.
7. Stoyan Zalmov, "Marco Rubio: 'It Was Not God's Plan That I Be President;' God Is 'Perfect and Makes No Mistakes,'" *Christian Post*, 16 Mar 2016, http://www.christianpost.com/news/marco-rubio-god-plan-president-perfect-florida-159287/.

81

BOBBY RUSH

US Representative from Illinois

Activism through the Word

The Spirit of the Lord is upon me because he has anointed me to preach the gospel to the poor; he has sent me to heal the brokenhearted, to proclaim liberty to the captives and recovery of sight to the blind, to set at liberty those that are broken, to proclaim the acceptable year of the Lord.

—Luke 4:18–19 (Jubilee Bible 2000)

Bobby Rush is a civil rights leader, the only politician to have ever defeated Barack Obama in an election (the 2000 Democratic primary for Illinois's first congressional district), and pastor of the Beloved Community Christian Church in the Englewood neighborhood of Chicago. He was radicalized in his younger years and cofounded the Illinois chapter of the Black Panther Party.

"I must admit that I was not always an ardent Bible reader," he said. "I was always in and around the church, but as so many of us who belong to church, I was in the church, but church wasn't in me."

Rush tells of being born-again, "I am an activist, and for years I had shunned this Bible because it didn't speak to my activism. And then the Holy Spirit spoke to me through my conversations and through my interests in reading the Bible."

He tells of two scriptures especially influencing him. In the Old Testament it was Micah 6:6–8, where the Lord simply asks humanity to "love mercy and to walk humbly with your God." In the New Testament it was Luke 4:18–19 (quoted above). "In those words, it encapsulated all that I had attempted to be," he said, "my activism, my love for humanity and my love for the Lord."

"I have been renewed as a man by the renewing of my mind according to the dictates and the Spirit that's incorporated in the reading of the Bible," said the congressman. "I am a changed man; I am a new man. I don't have the same friends I used to have. I don't walk the same way; I don't talk the same way, and it's all because of this Bible."[1]

NOTE

1. Congressional Record, 110th Congress, 1st Session, Issue: Vol. 153, No. 170, 5 Nov 2007, https://www.congress.gov/congressional-record/2007/11/05/house-section/article/H12484-1.

82

PAUL RYAN

Speaker of the US House of Representatives

Grace through the God of Peace

Now the God of peace, who brought up from the dead the great Shepherd of the sheep through the blood of the eternal covenant, even Jesus our Lord, equip you in every good thing to do His will, working in us that which is pleasing in His sight, through Jesus Christ, to whom be the glory forever and ever. Amen.

—Hebrews 13:20–21 (NASB)

A congressman from Wisconsin, Ryan was the Republican nominee for vice president in 2012 as Mitt Romney's running mate and served as the fifty-fourth Speaker of the United States House of Representatives.

When in his home state, he still attends St. John Vianney Catholic Church in Janesville, where he was an altar boy as a youth. But despite his devout Catholicism of today and his youth, Ryan had a period in his life when he questioned God.

As a sixteen-year-old boy, he walked into the house one day to find his fifty-five-year-old father dead from alcoholism. The tragedy caused Ryan to stop going to Mass for the most part through his college years and early twenties, and to simply go through the motions when he did.

"I could list the holy days of obligation and detail the Gospels. I could recite the Act of Contrition on command and knew the Apostle's Creed by heart. But of course, saying the words and feeling the meaning behind them are two very different things," he said.

"Losing my dad was brutal for my whole family, and I can't say that the experience inclined my heart much toward faith," Ryan said. "In high school, I had tried to resolve the dissonance I felt by reading about different beliefs. I learned about all kinds of organized religions. I studied the writings of existentialists and atheists. But no matter the faith or philosophical position, my spiritual journey always brought me back to that same place where most everyone has been at one time or another: I believed in God, but I was mad at God."

In 1996, Ryan was a political aide to Kansas congressman Sam Brownback, an evangelical who was investigating Catholicism. Driving around the Sunflower State, they had many religious conversations. "Having a non-Catholic asking me serious questions about Church doctrine was an important responsibility," Ryan said. "I took that seriously, and our talks became the catalyst for a deepening of my faith. At Sam's urging, I dove a little more into the writings of C. S. Lewis. By my mid-twenties, I started attending Mass again. Sam kept searching and eventually converted to Catholicism himself."

Today, Ryan is devout in his belief, and he's not shy to discuss God, scriptures, and faith with others. In fact, by discussing their spiritual lives, Mitt Romney grew close to Ryan, eventually choosing him as a running mate. "We talked about faith—my Catholicism, his Mormonism," Ryan said.[1] He learned a few things about the Latter-day Saints, and later at an event honoring Sen. Orrin Hatch, he shared Latter-day Saint scripture: "In the Book of Mormon, King Benjamin says, 'I tell you these things that ye may learn wisdom, that ye may learn that when ye are in the service of your fellow beings ye are only in the service of your God,'" Ryan said, quoting Mosiah 2:17.[2]

At a Catholic Prayer Breakfast in 2016, Ryan shared his view of God, echoing the words of Hebrews 13. "Every good work is the work of God. It is His grace working inside us," he said. "And when you realize that, you not only lose your pride, you lose your sense of despair. I believe that's the meaning of true happiness—at least in this world. It is not a cheap thrill or temporary exuberance: It is a deep, abiding inner peace. And what gives us that peace is coming to know God."[3]

NOTES

1. Mark Stricherz, "Rep. Paul Ryan, Former VP Candidate, Writes about Faith Journey," *Newsmax,* 4 Sep 2014, http://www.newsmax.com/Politics/Paul-Ryan-Catholicism-book-The-Way-Forward/2014/09/04/id/592692/.
2. Ben Lockhart, "Sen. Orrin Hatch Honored as Giant in Our City," *Deseret News,* 9 Jun 2018, https://www.deseretnews.com/article/900021190/sen-orrin-hatch-honored-as-giant-in-our-city.html.
3. Paul Ryan, Catholic Prayer Breakfast, May 2016, quoted in Virginia Foxx, *God Is in the House: Congressional Testimonies of Faith* (Salt Lake City: Ensign Peak, 2016), x.

83

BERNIE SANDERS

US Senator from Vermont

Treating Others Humanely

So in everything, do to others what you would have them do to you, for this sums up the Law and the Prophets.

—Matthew 7:12 (NIV)

Despite going further than any Jewish candidate for president, the scripture that Bernie Sanders repeatedly quoted on the 2016 campaign trail for the Democratic nomination was not from the Torah or Talmud, but rather, from the Christian New Testament.

"I am far, far from a perfect human being," he said in a speech at Liberty University, "but I am motivated by a vision which exists in all of the great religions—Christianity, Judaism, Islam, Buddhism and others—and which is so beautifully and clearly stated in Matthew 7:12. 'So in everything, do to others what you would have them to do to you, for this sums up the Law and the prophets.' The Golden Rule. Do to others what you would have them do to you. Not very complicated."[1]

This is just one of the many times the socialist senator quoted the Golden Rule during the campaign. He also demonstrated great admiration for Pope Francis on numerous occasions. "I am deeply impressed by the teachings of this pope," he said. "He has shined a light for all the world to see, that we cannot continue to tolerate the kind of greed and selfishness that we are seeing in the global economy." But just because he quotes the Gospels and admires the pope doesn't mean that Sanders has left the faith of his fathers for Christianity.

"I am not actively involved in organized religion," Sanders has said, but that doesn't mean the Independent senator isn't spiritual. "You know, every-one practices religion in a different way. To me, I would not be here tonight, I would not be running for president of the United States if I did not have very strong religious and spiritual feelings." While not very public about that spirituality, Sanders doesn't deny its influence. "It's a guiding principle in my life, absolutely," he said.[2]

His father fled anti-Semitism in Poland, coming to America in 1921. The Jewish Sanders family did hold traditional Passover seders but rarely attended synagogue. He learned of the prophets and patriarchs studying the Torah at a Hebrew school located at an Orthodox synagogue, and after college he even spent some time on a kibbutz in northern Israel. However, being on the collective farm in the Holy Land did more to solidify his socialist views than flame his religious fervor.[3]

Even though he is not actively practicing the rites and rituals of Judaism, Sanders still draws strength and identity from his heritage. "I am very proud to be Jewish, and being Jewish is so much of what I am," he told Anderson Cooper in a CNN interview. "Look, my father's family was wiped out by Hitler in the Holocaust. I know about what crazy and radical and extremist politics mean," Sanders said. "I learned that lesson as a tiny, tiny child when my mother would take me shopping and we would see people working in stores who had numbers on their arms because they were in Hitler's concen-tration camps. I am very proud of being Jewish, and that is an essential part of who I am as a human being."[4]

In a revealing moment, Sanders was asked on *Jimmy Kimmel Live* about his religiosity. "You say you're culturally Jewish, but you don't feel religious. Do you believe in God, and do you think that's important to the people of the United States?"

"I am who I am, and what I believe in and what my spirituality is about is that we're all in this together," Sanders answered, and then he once again channeled Matthew 7:12. "I think it is not a good thing to believe as human beings we can turn our backs on the suffering of other people."[5]

NOTES

1. Ross Barken, "Bernie Sanders Quotes From the Bible at Liberty University," *Observer*, 14 Sep 2015, http://observer.com/2015/09/bernie-sanders-quotes-from-the-bible-at-liberty -university.
2. Daniel Burke, "The Book of Bernie: Inside Sanders' unorthodox faith," *CNN*, 15 Apr 2016, http://www.cnn.com/2016/04/14/politics/bernie-sanders-religion/index.html.
3. Ibid.
4. Yehiel Poupko, "Is Bernie Sanders Religious?," *Christianity Today*, 2 Jun 2016, http://www .christianitytoday.com/ct/2016/june-web-only/is-bernie-sanders-religious.html?start=2.
5. Ismat Sarah Mangla, "Is Bernie Sanders Jewish? Candidate Invokes 'Spirituality' When Asked about God on 'Jimmy Kimmel Live,'" *International Business Times*, 22 Oct 2015, http://www .ibtimes.com/bernie-sanders-jewish-candidate-invokes-spirituality-when-asked-about-god -jimmy-2152474.

84

CHUCK SCHUMER

US Senate Minority Leader

Welcoming the Stranger

You shall not wrong a stranger or oppress him, for you were strangers in the land of Egypt.

—*Exodus 22:21 (NASB)*

Charles Schumer grew up in a Jewish family, whose ancestors were from Ukraine. Representing cosmopolitan New York in the Senate, the Democrat has been elected the first Jewish Minority Leader in Senate history.

Schumer lashed out against President Donald Trump's executive order temporarily banning immigrants from seven Muslim-majority nations in January 2017. The ban is "mean spirited and un-American," he said. "These orders go against what America has always been about."[1]

In the same press event, the senator quoted the Torah. "It admonishes us not to wrong or oppress a stranger," he said of Exodus 22, "for you were strangers in the land of Egypt." The Jewish senator also quoted a Christian scripture in Matthew: "I was hungry and you gave me something to eat," he read. "I was a stranger and you invited me in."[2]

NOTES

1. Lilly Maier, "Chuck Schumer Tears Up over Muslim Ban," *Forward*, 30 Jan 2017, http:// forward.com/news/361560/watch-chuck-schumer-tears-up-over-muslim-ban/.
2. "Sen. Schumer Quotes Scripture and the Pope," *C-SPAN*, 29 Jan 2017, https://www.cspan .org/video/?c4653304/sen-schumer-quotes-scripture-pope.

85

TIM SCOTT

US Senator from South Carolina

Love through Jesus

Love your neighbor as yourself.

—Matthew 22:39 (NIV)

Tim Scott made history as the first African-American senator from South Carolina and became the first black Republican elected from the South since 1881, four years after Reconstruction. When first appointed to fill a vacancy in the Senate, he thanked his "Lord and Savior Jesus Christ."[1]

After all, Scott has been a devout Christian since his college days at Presbyterian College. He learned to love the Bible at Fellowship of Christian Athletes meetings. "I just dove into the scriptures and started memorizing different scriptures and started becoming as much as possible a part of the scripture. I wanted it to be grafted into my heart," Scott said.[2]

He made the personal decision to dedicate his life to Jesus Christ. "I remember walking down the aisle, and I got down on my knees as a person who is so selfish," he said of his baptism, "but when I rose back up the Lord had become the Master of my life."[3]

Today, Scott is a devout evangelical and a member of Seacoast Church in Charleston, where he has served on the church's board. He weaves Bible verses into his campaign stump speech on occasion. "Ethics reform, according to the Book of James, is at a higher level for leaders and I think it should be," he said at a Myrtle Beach Tea Party meeting, for example.[4]

"There's an old Scripture in the Book of Matthew that says love your neighbor," he said in an interview on the eve of the 2017 presidential inauguration. "Now, I would hope we as leaders would look for ways to bring this country together—from the president of the United States down to every member of Congress, to leaders of households and at the state level as well."[5]

NOTES

1. Michael Warren, "Tim Scott Appointed to U.S. Senate," *Weekly Standard,* 17 Dec 2012, http://www.weeklystandard.com/tim-scott-appointed-us-senate/article/689900.
2. David Brody, "Tea Party's Scott: I'm Not 'The Black Republican,'" *CBN News,* 26 Dec 2012, http://www.cbn.com/cbnnews/politics/2010/september/tea-partys-tim-scott-im-not-the-black-republican/?mobile=false.
3. "Tim Scott Quotes," *BrainyQuote,* retrieved 28 Aug 2017, https://www.brainyquote.com/quotes/quotes/t/timscott629332.html.
4. Brody, "Tea Party's Scott."
5. Ryan Struyk, "Sen. Tim Scott: Conservatives Could Be 'Equally Unhappy' with Trump," *ABC 13,* 20 Jan 2017, http://abc13.com/news/sen-tim-scott-conservatives-could-be-equally-unhappy-with-trump/1710863.

86

STEVE SOUTHERLAND II

Congressman from Florida

Live by the Faith

I am crucified with Christ: nevertheless I live, yet not I, but Christ liveth in me: and the life which I now live in the flesh I live by the faith of the Son of God, who loved me, and gave himself for me.

—Galatians 2:20 (KJV)

The owner and president of a funeral home who has comforted count-less families mourning loved ones, Steve Southerland II is also a devout Southern Baptist. As a member of Congress, the Republican encouraged people to have faith and to embrace work, especially as a champion of food-stamp reform.

Southerland preached what he called the "Gospel of Work." He said once to a group at a job-training program preparing for jobs after living on welfare, "Work is life. Work is opportunity." He invoked the biblical book of Genesis, recalling how God charged Adam to work and tend the Garden of Eden. "Even in paradise, we worked," he said. "Work is not a punishment. It is what connects you with your purpose in life. What's your purpose?"[1]

On another occasion, the Christian congressman was asked what his favorite scripture was. "There are several verses that are very important to me," he replied, "one of which is Galatians 2:20 [quoted above]. . . . I hope the same can be said of me. I want to be faithful, and I find that we must fight for our cause."[2]

NOTES

1. Eli Saslow, "Hard work: A Florida Republican pushing to overhaul the food stamp system toils to win over a divided Congress," *Washington Post*, 24 Sep 2013, http://www.washingtonpost.com/sf/national/2013/09/24/hard-work/?utm_term=.9c68a6140760.
2. Virginia Foxx, *God Is in the House: Congressional Testimonies of Faith* (Salt Lake City: Ensign Peak, 2016), 59–60.

87

WILLIAM HOWARD TAFT

Twenty-Seventh President of the United States

Discernment and Judgment

Give therefore thy servant an understanding heart to judge thy people, that I may discern between good and bad: for who is able to judge this thy so great a people?

And the speech pleased the Lord, that Solomon had asked this thing.

And God said unto him, Because thou hast asked this thing, and hast not asked for thyself long life; neither hast asked riches for thyself, nor hast asked the life of thine enemies; but hast asked for thyself understanding to discern judgment.

—*1 Kings 3:9–11 (KJV)*

Taft liked the teachings of the Bible, but like his predecessor Jefferson, he questioned the miracles in the book and rejected the idea of Jesus as the Son of God. "I am a Unitarian. I believe in God," he said. "I do not believe in the divinity of Christ, and there are many other of the postulates of the orthodox creed to which I cannot subscribe. I am not, however, a scoffer at religion but on the contrary recognize, in the fullest manner, the elevating influence that it has had and always will have in the history of mankind."[1]

Skeptics of the new president consequently wondered if he would even place his hand on a Bible for his inauguration. But the large president-elect did. He even added the customary "So help me God" at the end of the oath and picked up the Bible in both hands and kissed it.[2]

Like McKinley, the Republican Taft chose the plea of King Solomon, praying for wisdom, as the scripture to be sworn in on. However, while McKinley picked the version from Chronicles, Taft selected the account in Kings (quoted above).[3]

NOTES

1. "God in the White House," *PBS*, retrieved 4 Apr 2017, http://www.pbs.org/godinamerica/god-in-the-white-house.
2. John C. McCollister, *God and the Oval Office* (Nashville: W Publishing Group, 2005), 135.
3. "The 31st Presidential Inauguration," Joint Congressional Committee on Inaugural Ceremonies, retrieved 11 Apr 2017, https://www.inaugural.senate.gov/about/past-inaugural-ceremonies/31st-inaugural-ceremonies.

88

ZACHARY TAYLOR

Tenth President of the United States

Blossom as the Rose

The wilderness and the solitary place shall be glad for them; and the desert shall rejoice, and blossom as the rose.

—*Isaiah 35:1 (KJV)*

Not particularly religious, "Old Rough and Ready" (as President Taylor was nicknamed) rarely attended church, yet "he was a constant reader of the Bible," said his daughter Betty Taylor Bliss, "and practiced all its precepts, acknowledging his responsibility to God."[1]

Taylor was impressed with the way the Bible had guided America's founders. "It was the love of the truths of this great Book that our fathers abandoned their native shores for the wilderness," he said, a nod to the Pilgrims, Puritans, Quakers, Catholics, and others who came to the American colonies for religious freedoms. "Animated by its lofty principles, they toiled and suffered till the desert blossomed as the rose [Isaiah 35:1]."

He went on to say, "The Bible is the best of books and I wish it were in the hands of everyone. It is indispensable to the safety and permanence of our institution; a free government cannot exist without religion and morals, and there cannot be morals without religion, nor religion without the Bible."

He wanted to see the Good Book in the hands of youth. "Especially should the Bible be placed in the hands of the young," Taylor said. "It is the best school book in the world . . . I would that all of our people were brought up under the influence of that Holy Book."[2]

NOTES

1. John C. McCollister, *God and the Oval Office* (Nashville: W Publishing Group, 2005), 60.
2. "The President and the Bible," *New York Semi-Weekly Tribune*, 9 May 1849, Vol. IV, No. 100, p. 1.

89

CLARENCE THOMAS

US Supreme Court Justice

Embracing Faith

Hope does not disappoint, because the love of God has been poured out into our hearts through the Holy Spirit that has been given to us.

For Christ, though we were still helpless, died at the appointed time for the ungodly.

Indeed, only with difficulty does one die for a just person, though perhaps for a good person, one might even find courage to die.

But God proves his love for us in that while we were still sinners, Christ died for us.

How much more then, since we are now justified by his blood, will we be saved through him from the wrath.

Indeed, if, while we were enemies, we were reconciled to God through the death of his Son, how much more, once reconciled, will we be saved by his life.

Not only that, but we also boast of God through our Lord Jesus Christ, through whom we have now received reconciliation.

—*Romans 5:5–11 (New American Bible Revised Edition)*

The second African-American to serve on the United States Supreme Court, Clarence Thomas, has attended numerous denominations throughout his life and is presently a Roman Catholic.

He was born into a Baptist family, but he converted to Catholicism while in the second grade. He was an altar boy and attended Catholic schools. For some of his upbringing, however, he was raised by a Seventh-day Adventist grandmother and attended that church with her for years.

For a time, young Clarence Thomas was interested in becoming a priest, and he attended Saint John Vianney Seminary in Georgia and Immaculate Conception Seminary in Missouri. He later attended College of the Holy Cross in Massachusetts. He left the Catholic Church and his path to become a priest on the day Martin Luther King Jr. was shot in 1968. "I hope the S.O.B. dies," said a white fellow seminarian to Thomas, disgusting him enough to leave. Thomas later affiliated with a charismatic Episcopal church in Virginia.

In 1996, Thomas returned to what he called the "precious gift" of his Catholic faith. "It was a joy to receive my first Communion in St. Joseph Chapel this afternoon," he said after twenty-eight years of estrangement. This made him the third Catholic on the Supreme Court, and he was often seen walking to the court after attending Mass with fellow Catholic Justice Antonin Scalia.[1]

Perhaps it was appropriate, then, that Thomas was asked to share a scripture at the funeral of his friend and fellow justice and believer when Scalia passed away in February 2016. In front of friends and family of the deceased gathered at the Basilica of the National Shrine of the Immaculate Conception in Washington, DC, Thomas stood and said in his deep voice, "A reading from the letter of Saint Paul to the Romans," and then read the comforting verses from Romans 5:5–11 (quoted above). "The Word of the Lord," he said after he read the verses.[2]

In a commencement address given at Hillsdale College in Michigan just a few months later, Thomas encouraged the graduates to be proud of their faith. "Do not hide your faith and your beliefs under a bushel basket, especially in this world that seems to have gone mad with political correctness," he said, paraphrasing Matthew 5:15.

"In today's world of political correctness, specific rights for every individual sect, and the gradual push to ban what is viewed as discriminating religious viewpoints," he said, "it is important to remember what God planned for our lives and what we are meant to do on earth."[3]

NOTES

1. "The Religious Affiliation of Supreme Court Justice Clarence Thomas," *Adherents.com,* 30 Jan 2006, http://www.adherents.com/people/pt/Clarence_Thomas.html.

2. "Clarence Thomas: Reading of Holy Scripture at the Funeral Mass of Christian Burial for Antonin Scalia," *American Rhetoric Online Speech Bank,* 20 Feb 2016, https://www.americanrhetoric.com/speeches/clarencethomasscripturereading.htm.

3. Kenya Sinclair, "'Do not hide your faith and your beliefs': Justice Thomas warns against political correctness," *Catholic Online,* 16 May 2016, http://www.catholic.org/news/politics/story.php?id=68953.

90

HARRY S. TRUMAN

Thirty-Third President of the United States

The Practical Gospel

Blessed are the poor in spirit: for theirs is the kingdom of heaven.

Blessed are they that mourn: for they shall be comforted.

Blessed are the meek: for they shall inherit the earth.

Blessed are they which do hunger and thirst after righteousness: for they shall be filled.

Blessed are the merciful: for they shall obtain mercy.

Blessed are the pure in heart: for they shall see God.

Blessed are the peacemakers: for they shall be called the children of God.

Blessed are they which are persecuted for righteousness' sake: for theirs is the kingdom of heaven.

Blessed are ye, when men shall revile you, and persecute you, and shall say all manner of evil against you falsely, for my sake.

—Matthew 5:3–11 (KJV)

Truman was raised in a Baptist family and claimed to have read the Bible all the way through twice before starting school.[1] A practical man, he appreciated the Ten Commandments and the Beatitudes. In fact, in his 1949 inaugural, he was sworn in on two Bibles, and he had one turned to the Beatitudes in Matthew 5 and the other Bible opened to the Ten Commandments in Exodus.[2]

"The fundamental basis of this nation's laws was given to Moses on the Mount," Truman once said. "The fundamental basis of our Bill of Rights comes from the teachings we get from Exodus and Saint Matthew, from Isaiah and Saint Paul."[3]

But the verses of the Beatitudes shared in the Sermon on the Mount seemed to be his favorite. "The Sermon on the Mount is the greatest of all things in the Bible," the Democrat from Missouri once said, "a way of life, and maybe someday men will get to understand it as the *real* way of life."[4]

NOTES

1. "God in the White House," *PBS*, retrieved 4 Apr 2017, http://www.pbs.org/godinamerica /god-in-the-white-house/.
2. "The 41st Presidential Inauguration," Joint Congressional Committee on Inaugural Ceremonies, retrieved 11 Apr 2017, https://www.inaugural.senate.gov/about/past-inaugural -ceremonies/41st-inaugural-ceremonies/.
3. Tim George, "American Presidents and the Bible," *Off the Grid News*, retrieved 21 Mar 2017, http://www.offthegridnews.com/misc/american-presidents-and-the-bible/.
4. John C. McCollister, *God and the Oval Office* (Nashville: W Publishing Group, 2005), 169.

91

DONALD J. TRUMP

Forty-Fifth President of the United States

A Wise Man Is Strong

Be not thou envious against evil men, neither desire to be with them.

For their heart studieth destruction, and their lips talk of mischief.

Through wisdom is an house builded; and by understanding it is established:

And by knowledge shall the chambers be filled with all precious and pleasant riches.

A wise man is strong; yea, a man of knowledge increaseth strength.

For by wise counsel thou shalt make thy war: and in multitude of counsellors there is safety.

—Proverbs 24:1–6 (KJV)

D onald Trump was raised by his Lutheran father and Presbyterian mother. He describes himself as a mainline Protestant, and when sworn in as president he did so on both the Lincoln Bible and the Bible he received in 1955 when he completed Sunday Church Primary School as a boy at the First Presbyterian Church in Jamaica, Queens.[1]

"My mother gave me this Bible. This very Bible many years ago," Trump said of his family Bible. "In fact, it's her writing, right here. She wrote the name and my address, and it's just very special to me."[2]

During his presidential campaign, it was clear that Trump was not nearly as devout in his faith as most presidents, but he took great pains to share his admiration of scripture. "I've said it before—I think the Bible is the most important book ever written—not even close," he said. "People like to give me Bibles, which I love."[3]

He compared the Bible to an epic motion picture. "I don't like to use this analogy, but like a great movie, a great, incredible movie. You'll see it once, it will be good. You'll see it again. You can see it twenty times, and every time you'll appreciate it more. The Bible is the most special thing."[4]

Trump, like many of his predecessors, also acknowledged that the values from the Bible have been critical to America's heritage. "The fact is that our deep-rooted religious beliefs made this country great," he said. "That belief in the lessons of the Bible has had a lot to do with our growth and success."[5]

In August 2015, when candidate Trump was asked by Bloomberg what his favorite verse was, he demurred. "I wouldn't want to get into it. Because to me, that's very personal," he said. "The Bible means a lot to me, but I don't want to get into specifics."[6]

The following month in an interview with David Brody, Trump did get a little more specific. "There's so many things that you can learn from it [the Bible]. Proverbs, the chapter 'never bend to envy.' I've had that thing all of my life where people are bending to envy."[7] Critics pounced on this, claiming such a verse does not exist, but the Trump campaign emailed the clarification that he was referring to Proverbs 24 (quoted above).[8]

"Proverbs 24 teaches that envy should be replaced with discernment. Wisdom builds and understanding establishes, whether it be a family, a house, or our community," Trump wrote. "For me, this is important, especially in this race for President of the United States as it shows it is important to rely on one's own wisdom and ability rather than follow others down the wrong path."[9]

In January 2016, candidate Trump spoke at Liberty University, where he took some heat in mispronouncing the book where the university's official scripture comes from. "Two Corinthians, right? 3:17, that's the whole ballgame," Trump said, mispronouncing "Second Corinthians." He continued, paraphrasing the verse: "Where the spirit of the Lord, right . . . there is liberty. Here, there is liberty . . . Liberty University, but it is so true."

A few months later in a radio interview with Bob Lonsberry on WHAM 1180 AM, Trump was asked once again if there was a favorite Bible verse or story that has influenced him. "Well, I think many. I mean, when we get into the Bible, I think many, so many. And some people, look, an eye for an eye, you can almost say that," Trump said, referring to the Mosaic law of justice outlined in Exodus 21. "That's not a particularly nice thing," he explained. "But you know, if you look at what's happening to our country, I mean, when you see what's going on with our country, how people are taking advantage of us, and how they scoff at us and laugh at us. And they laugh at our face, and they're taking our jobs, they're taking our money, they're taking the health of our country. And we have to be very firm and have to be very strong. And we can learn a lot from the Bible, that I can tell you."[10]

Trump quoted scripture on a number of other occasions, including in September 2016 while speaking to an African-American congregation in Detroit. "I'd like to conclude with a passage from 1 John, chapter 4," he said at the end of his remarks. "You know it? See, most groups I speak to don't know that. But we know it. If you want, we can say it together: 'No one has ever seen God, but if we love one another, God lives in us and His love is made complete in us.' And that is so true."

And as a newly sworn-in president, Donald Trump referenced scripture once again, this time quoting Psalm 133:1. "The Bible tells us how good and pleasant it is when God's people live together in unity," he said, "whether we are black or brown or white, we all bleed the same red blood of patriots."[11]

NOTES

1. Meghan Murphy-Gill, "The Faith of Donald Trump," *U.S. Catholic*, 19 Jan 2017, http://www .uscatholic.org/articles/201701/faith-donald-trump-30910. See also R. Scott Hanson, "Donald Trump, God and the Depth of Faith," *Time*, 22 Jan 2017, http://time.com/4642696/donald -trump-god-faith.
2. Holly Meyer, "What Bible Did Donald Trump Use on Inauguration Day?" *Tennessean*, 17 Jan 2017,http://www.tennessean.com/story/news/religion/2017/01/17/donald-trump-sworn-lincoln -family-bibles/96387086.
3. Donald Trump, *Crippled America: How to Make America Great Again* (New York: Threshold Editions, 2015), 130.
4. David Brody, "Donald Trump Talks about the Bible and Book of Proverbs," *CBN News*, 16 Sep 2015, http://www1.cbn.com/thebrodyfile/archive/2015/09/16/brody-file-video-exclusive -donald-trump-talks-about-the-bible.
5. Trump, *Crippled America*, 131.
6. Eugene Scott, "Trump says Bible is his favorite book, but declines to share favorite verse," *CNN*, 27 Aug 2015, http://www.cnn.com/2015/08/27/politics/donald-trump-favorite-bible -verses/.
7. Brody, "Donald Trump Talks."

8. Jenna Johnson, "Donald Trump clears up confusion about his favorite Bible verse," *Washington Post,* 17 Sep 2015, https://www.washingtonpost.com/news/post-politics/wp/2015/09/17/donald-trump-clears-up-confusion-about-his-favorite-bible-verse/?utm_term=.aeaa4a4a83dd.

9. David Brody, "Donald Trump's Email on Proverbs 24," *CBN News,* 17 Sep 2015, http://www1.cbn.com/thebrodyfile/archive/2015/09/17/only-on-brody-file-donald-trumps-email-on-proverbs-24.

10. Rebecca Shabad, "Donald Trump Names His Favorite Bible Verse," *CBS News,* 14 Apr 2016, http://www.cbsnews.com/news/donald-trump-names-his-favorite-bible-verse.

11. Hanson, "Donald Trump, God and the Depth of Faith."

92

MELANIA TRUMP

First Lady of the United States

Peace through Prayer

Our Father who art in heaven, hallowed be thy name; thy kingdom come; thy will be done on earth as it is in heaven.

Give us this day our daily bread; and forgive us our trespasses as we forgive those who trespass against us; and lead us not into temptation, but deliver us from evil.

For thine is the kingdom, and the power, and the glory; for ever and ever,

Amen.

—Matthew 6:9–13 (1928 Book of Common Prayer)

Melania Trump is not only the first foreign-born First Lady since John Quincy Adams's wife, Louisa, who was born in London, but she is also the first Roman Catholic resident of the White House since the Kennedys.

Trump surprised an audience gathered in Melbourne, Florida, in February 2017, when she began the rally saying, "Let us pray," and reciting the Lord's Prayer (as quoted above). She said afterward to the cheering crowd, "I will always stay true to myself, and be truthful to you."[1]

Praying the "Our Father" like she did at that rally is true to herself as a practicing Roman Catholic. Even though she is married to a Presbyterian president and they were wed in an Episcopal church in Florida, Melania Trump has been a Catholic since her childhood in Slovenia. However, because her father was a Communist Party official, she was not baptized as a child and could not outwardly practice her faith until after the fall of the Iron Curtain.

She thrilled in May 2017 to meet with Pope Francis at the Vatican, appearing before the Holy Father in traditional modesty—a long-sleeved black dress with a black mantilla covering her head. "Today's visit with His Holiness Pope Francis is one I'll never forget," she tweeted. "I was humbled by the honor. Blessings to all."

Prayer is important to Melania Trump, and during her visit with the Pope, she had him bless a set of rosary beads. Earlier in the day, she had prayed before a statue of the Virgin Mary at a children's hospital in Rome. She also stopped to pray in the hospital's chapel.[2] Whether in Italy or Florida, the First Lady has demonstrated the importance of prayer in her life.

NOTES

1. William Steakin, "Melania Opens President Trump's Campaign Rally with Lord's Prayer," *AOL.com,* 18 Feb 2017, https://www.aol.com/article/news/2017/02/18/melania-opens-pres ident-trumps-campaign-rally-with-lords-praye/21716918/.
2. Cavan Sieczkowski, "Melania Trump Will Be the First Catholic to Live at the White House Since JFK," *Huffington Post,* 25 May 2017, http://www.huffingtonpost.com/entry/melania -trump-catholic-white-house_us_59270d0ce4b0265790f5f76f. See also David Martosko, "Melania Trump Reveals She Is Catholic," *Daily Mail,* 24 May 2017, http://www.dailymail .co.uk/news/article-4539392/Melania-Catholic-White-House-Kennedy.html.

93

HARRIET TUBMAN

Abolitionist and Political Activist

Leading Them out of Bondage

I am the Lord thy God, which have brought thee out of the land of Egypt, out of the house of bondage.

—*Exodus 20:2 (KJV)*

Raised in bondage on a plantation in Maryland, Harriet Tubman developed faith in Jesus Christ as her Savior as she learned Bible stories from her mother, who was a cook in "the big house." While she never learned to read, Tubman had a terrific memory and would memorize and often quote long passages of scripture.

In 1849, when she was in her late twenties, she escaped the plantation by herself and then found support from several Quakers affiliated with the Underground Railroad. "Oh, how I prayed then," she said of that week traveling north ninety miles to Pennsylvania, "lying on the cold, damp ground, 'Oh, dear Lord, I ain't got no friend but you. Come to my help, Lord, for I'm in trouble!'"[1]

Tubman claimed to hear the voice of God throughout the rest of her life and to be guided often by visions. She not only reached the free states, but she then went south again thirteen times in her life to help slaves escape to the North. Some historians estimate she helped as many as three hundred escape to freedom. Like Moses of old, Harriet Tubman was determined to lead as many people as possible "from the land of Egypt, from the house of bondage," she said, quoting Exodus.[2]

"On my underground railroad, I never run my train off the track and I never lose a passenger," Tubman said. Her "passengers" would hear her often speak of "consulting with God," and when they were surprised by some miraculous scene of deliverance, Tubman would reply, "Don't, I tell you, Missus. It wasn't me. It was the Lord!"[3]

NOTES

1. Mark Ellis, "Harriet Tubman Followed the Voice of God," *God Reports*, 28 Apr 2016, http://blog.godreports.com/2016/04/harriet-tubman-she-followed-the-voice-of-god/.
2. Rebecca Price Janney, "People of Faith: Harriet Tubman," *Crosswalk.com*, 21 Feb 2003, https://www.crosswalk.com/faith/spiritual-life/people-of-faith-harriet-tubman-1186786.html.
3. Ellis, "Harriet Tubman Followed the Voice of God."

94

SCOTT WALKER

Governor of Wisconsin

All This through Him

I can do all this through him who gives me strength.

—*Philippians 4:13 (NIV)*

The son of a Baptist minister, Scott Walker grew up close to the church as his father ministered to congregations in Colorado, Iowa, and Wisconsin. Sometimes, Walker would even preach the sermon for his father. To earn his Eagle Scout award, Walker led his troop in a project to stop erosion above the church.[1]

Walker was baptized in the American Baptist Church at age thirteen. He viewed the event as a critical point in his life. "Lord, I'm ready . . . I'm ready to say—not just in front of my church, in front of the whole world—but I most importantly say at the foot of your throne that I'm ready to follow you each and every day," he said of how he felt at the time.

Today, Walker and his wife enjoy Bible reading groups. They attend Meadowbrook Church, which is part of the Elmbrook Church, a conservative, non-denominational evangelical megachurch. "Overall, my faith drives who I am and how I live," Walker told the *Milwaukee Journal Sentinel.* "My relationship with God drives every major decision in my life."[2]

As the Republican governor of Wisconsin, he tweeted in 2014 the scripture Philippians 4:13 (quoted above). Church and state separatists blasted him for using his state Twitter account to share the verse and demanded he remove it. "The verse was part of a devotional he read that morning, which inspired him, and he chose to share it," explained his press secretary. The Tweet soared in popularity and became the second most popular one in the Twitterverse that week.[3]

NOTES

1. Trip Gabriel, "Scott Walker, a Pastor's Son, Runs on Faith as Iowa Beckons," *New York Times,* 25 Apr 2015, https://www.nytimes.com/2015/04/26/us/politics/scott-walker-runs-on-faith -as-iowa-nears.html?_r=0.
2. Daniel Bice and Annysa Johnson, "On campaign trail, Walker sheds light on influence of faith," *Milwaukee-Wisconsin Journal Sentinel,* 23 Apr 2015, http://archive.jsonline .com/news/statepolitics/on-campaign-trail-walker-sheds-light-on-influence-of-faith -b99483387z1-301175401.html/.
3. Billy Hallowell, "The Bible Verse That Could Land Scott Walker in a Major Battle with Atheists," *Blaze,* 19 Mar 2014, http://www.theblaze.com/news/2014/03/19/the-bible-verse -that-could-land-scott-walker-in-a-major-battle-with-atheists/.

95

ELIZABETH WARREN

US Senator from Massachusetts

Golden Rule

And the King shall answer and say unto them, Verily I say unto you, Inasmuch as ye have done it unto one of the least of these my brethren, ye have done it unto me.

—Matthew 25:40 (KJV)

I grew up in the Methodist church and taught Sunday school," said Warren, "and one of my favorite passages of scripture is, 'Inasmuch as ye have done it unto one of the least of these my brethren, ye have done it unto me,' Matthew 25:40."[1] She later shared this scripture on numerous occasions.

At the Democratic National Convention in 2012, Warren again quoted Matthew 25:40 and then explained, "The passage teaches about God in each of us, that we are bound to each other, and we are called to act—not to sit, not to wait—but to act, all of us together."

The DNC deputy director of faith outreach, Joshua Dickson, praised her inclusion of the scripture. "Her inclusion of Matthew 25:40 was another reminder of the important role people of faith and faith traditions continue to play in the Democratic Party and reflects the core value that she and the President [Obama] share."[2]

Warren, a Harvard professor, was elected a senator that November. She later talked about how during that campaign she attended Easter services and Passover seders with her husband, Bruce, looking for "moments of peace" in "an otherwise crazy life," she said. "It felt healing to be able, even for a short while, to focus on values and to be in touch with the spirit that moved me into this race."

She would bring a Bible to these church meetings. "I carried my King James Bible to services, the same one I'd carried since fourth grade," she said. "Sometimes the pastor called on me to speak. I'd never spoken to a whole congregation. But I talked about my favorite Bible verse, Matthew 25:40. Its message was very simple: The Lord calls us to action. It's what we DO that matters most."[3]

NOTES

1. "Elizabeth Warren Quotes," *BrainyQuote*, retrieved 25 Jun 2017, https://www.brainyquote .com/quotes/quotes/e/elizabethw449227.html.
2. Elizabeth Dias, "Democrats' Favorite Biblical Passage: Matthew 25," *Time*, 6 Sep 2012, http://swampland.time.com/2012/09/06/democrats-favorite-biblical-passage-matthew-25.
3. Elizabeth Warren, *A Fighting Chance* (New York: Metropolitan Books, 2014), 243.

96

GEORGE WASHINGTON

First President of the United States

Freedom and Enjoying One's Labors

But they shall sit every man under his vine and under his fig tree; and none shall make them afraid: for the mouth of the Lord of hosts hath spoken it.

—*Micah 4:4 (KJV)*

Washington quoted Micah 4:4 over forty times in his letters and journals, far more than any other verse he referenced. The idea of freedom from being badgered by others and enjoying the fruit of one's labor become so synonymous with the first president that in the modern musical *Hamilton* these lines are appropriately quoted by his character as he bids farewell to the presidency.

Washington drew on another verse from the Old Testament prophet Micah after the American Revolution when he wrote a victorious letter to the governors of each of the newly independent states. Looking back on the miraculous deliverance of the new nation, the general concluded with Micah 6:8: "He hath shewed thee, O man, what is good; and what doth the Lord require of thee, but to do justly, and to love mercy, and to walk humbly with thy God?" However, Washington changed the end of the verse slightly to read, "to do justice, love, mercy, and imitate the divine author of our blessed religion."[1]

Although some believe him to be a deist, the Father of our Country valued God's word revealed in scripture. He said, "Above all, the pure and benign light of Revelation has had a meliorating influence on mankind, and increased the blessings of society."[2] Washington even once said, "It is impossible to rightly govern the world without God and the Bible."[3]

NOTES

1. "The Washington Statue," *Philadelphia Faith and Freedom,* retrieved 21 Mar 2017, http://www.philadelphiafaithandfreedom.com/washingtonstatue.
2. Art Farstad, "The Bible and the Presidents," *Faith Alone Magazine,* retrieved 21 Mar 2017, https://faithalone.org/magazine/y1992/92feb1.html.
3. Tim George, "American Presidents and the Bible," *Off the Grid News,* retrieved 21 Mar 2017, http://www.offthegridnews.com/misc/american-presidents-and-the-bible/.

97

ALLEN WEST

US Congressman from Florida

Strength in the Lord

No weapon that is formed against thee shall prosper; and every tongue that shall rise against thee in judgment thou shalt condemn. This is the heritage of the servants of the Lord, and their righteousness is of me, saith the Lord.

—Isaiah 54:17 (KJV)

West was the first African-American Republican congressman from Florida since 1876, and he served twenty-two years in the United States Army, including deployments to Iraq and Afghanistan. A devout Christian, West looks to God and draws strength from the scriptures in discussing defending freedom.

"I often think about what it means to stand for right and what you have to go through to protect our freedoms," he said.

"Isaiah 54:17 tells us, 'No weapon that is formed against thee shall prosper; and every tongue that shall rise against thee in judgment thou shalt condemn. This is the heritage of the servants of the Lord, and their righteousness is of me, saith the Lord.' That verse hangs on my office wall to remind me of my duty as a servant of the Lord."[1]

West finds not just strength but also joy in his religion and believes that those with faith tend to live happier lives. "America has a Judeo-Christian faith heritage and promotes the free exercise of religion," he said. "However, it has been my experience in life that people who possess no deep faith are not happy. After all, as it says in Joshua chapter 24, 'As for me and my house, we will serve the Lord.'"[2]

NOTES

1. Virginia Foxx, *God Is in the House: Congressional Testimonies of Faith* (Salt Lake City: Ensign Peak, 2016), 41.
2. Hemant Mehta, "Former Congressman Allen West: 'People Who Possess No Deep Faith Are Not Happy,'" *Patheos,* 9 Oct 2013, http://www.patheos.com/blogs/friendlyatheist/2013/10 /09/former-congressman-allen-west-people-who-possess-no-deep-faith-are-not-happy.

98

WOODROW WILSON

Twenty-Eighth President of the United States

Judgment, Liberty, and Strength

And take not the word of truth utterly out of my mouth; for I have hoped in thy judgments.

So shall I keep thy law continually for ever and ever.

And I will walk at liberty: for I seek thy precepts.

I will speak of thy testimonies also before kings, and will not be ashamed.

—Psalm 119:43–46 (KJV)

God is our refuge and strength, a very present help in trouble.

Therefore will not we fear, though the earth be removed, and though the mountains be carried into the midst of the sea;

Though the waters thereof roar and be troubled, though the mountains shake with the swelling thereof. Selah.

—Psalm 46:1–3 (KJV)

Wilson was the son of a Presbyterian minister who had a lifetime love of the Bible. He studied the Bible each night before bed and had read and reread the Good Book so many times that the famed psychologist Sigmund Freud, a contemporary, said that the president "wore out two or three Bibles in the course of his life."[1]

In 1911, Wilson spoke about the Bible as "a book which reveals men unto themselves, not as creatures in bondage, not as men under human authority, not as those bidden to take counsel and command of any human source. It reveals every man to himself as a distinct moral agent, responsible not to men, not even to those men whom he has put over him in authority, but responsible through his own conscience to his Lord and Maker."[2]

When being sworn in as the twenty-eighth president, he gravitated toward the Psalms. In his first inauguration in 1913, he chose to use the same Bible he had used being sworn in as governor of New Jersey and had it opened to Psalm 119:43–46.[3] These verses speak of judgment, law, and liberty—all important themes for Wilson.

Verse 46 also spoke prophetically of bearing testimonies before kings unashamedly. Wilson would indeed become the first president to visit Europe, and he worked to advance his "moral diplomacy" to kings without shame—including Italy's King Victor Emmanuel III, Pope Benedict XV, British Prime Minister David Lloyd George, and French Prime Minister Georges Clemenceau. He received a Nobel Peace Prize for his work to advance peace and the League of Nations.

By the time Wilson was taking the oath of office for a second time in 1917, the world was in a darker place. World War I was raging, German submarines had already killed Americans aboard the sunk *Lusitania* and other ships, and two days before, the Zimmerman telegram was made public, showing Germany's proposal to give Mexico the states of Texas, Arizona, and New Mexico if they allied with them in fighting the United States.

In this troubled time, Wilson was drawn toward Psalm 46, placing his left hand on the Bible that was opened to it.[4] It speaks of God being a refuge and comfort in present trouble, where waters roar and are troubled. Surely these verses brought solace to President Wilson, mere weeks before the United States entered the Great War.

"The Bible is the one supreme source of revelation for the meaning of life, the nature of God, and spiritual nature and needs of men," the Democratic president once said. "It is the only guide of life which really leads the spirit in the way of peace and salvation. America was born a Christian nation.

America was born to exemplify that devotion to the elements of righteousness which are derived from the revelations of Holy Scripture."[5]

NOTES

1. John C. McCollister, *God and the Oval Office* (Nashville: W Publishing Group, 2005), 139.
2. "God in the White House," *PBS*, retrieved 4 Apr 2017, http://www.pbs.org/godinamerica/god-in-the-white-house.
3. "The 32nd Presidential Inauguration," Joint Congressional Committee on Inaugural Ceremonies, retrieved 11 Apr 2017, https://www.inaugural.senate.gov/about/past-inaugural-ceremonies/32nd-inaugural-ceremonies.
4. "The 33rd Presidential Inauguration," Joint Congressional Committee on Inaugural Ceremonies, retrieved 11 Apr 2017, https://www.inaugural.senate.gov/about/past-inaugural-ceremonies/33rd-inaugural-ceremonies.
5. Tim George, "American Presidents and the Bible," *Off the Grid News*, retrieved 21 Mar 2017, http://www.offthegridnews.com/misc/american-presidents-and-the-bible.

99

FRANK WOLF

Congressman from Virginia

Champion of Religious Liberties

Again I looked and saw all the oppression that was taking place under
the sun: I saw the tears of the oppressed—and they have no comforter;
power was on the side of their oppressors—and they have no comforter.

—*Ecclesiastes 4:1 (NIV)*

Having served in Congress for thirty-four consecutive years, Frank
Wolf was Virginia's longest-serving member of Congress. "As a fol-
lower of Jesus, I am called to work for justice and reconciliation, and to be
an advocate for those who cannot speak for themselves. I plan to focus my
future work on human rights and religious freedom—both domestic and
international—as well as matters of the culture and the American family,"
said Wolf, a Republican and faithful Presbyterian, upon retirement from the
House of Representatives.[1]

A champion of religious liberties, Wolf stood up for victims of the Darfur
genocide, warned about Christians being decimated by ISIS, spoke up for
the persecution of the Rohingya in Burma and the Ahmadi in Pakistan.

"Jesus didn't differentiate. If it's a Uighur in China, we all speak out. If it's a Catholic bishop in Hong Kong, we all speak out," he said.[2] The Frank R. Wolf International Religious Freedom Act was named for him and signed into law by President Barack Obama in 2016.

He indicated a favorite verse is Ecclesiastes 4:1 (quoted above). "I felt called to make these people—the poor, the hungry, the prisoner, and the oppressed—my mission," he said. "It is, quite frankly, what kept me in Congress so long, the desire to bring comfort—and sometimes power—to those who suffer. It is a cause we must continue to fight for, one that we must promote as we select new men and women to represent us in Congress."[3]

Notes

1. "Frank Wolf Quotes," *BrainyQuote*, retrieved 2 Sep 2017, https://www.brainyquote.com/quotes/quotes/f/frankwolf651488.html.
2. Bridget Johnson, "House Loses a Human-Rights Champion—But Don't Call Frank Wolf 'Retired,'" *PJ Media*, 5 Jan 2015, https://pjmedia.com/blog/house-loses-a-human-rights-champion-but-dont-call-frank-wolf-retired/.
3. Virginia Foxx, *God Is in the House: Congressional Testimonies of Faith* (Salt Lake City: Ensign Peak, 2016), 77–78.

100

RON WYDEN

US Senator from Oregon

Wisdom from Any Source

Have them bring every major dispute to you but let them decide every minor dispute for themselves. Make it easier for yourself by letting them share the burden with you.

—*Exodus 18:21 (New Jewish Publication Society Translation of the Torah)*

The senior senator from Oregon was born to Jewish refugees who had fled Nazi Germany, and he has been deeply influenced by his Jewish heritage. "My parents told me at a young age what it was like to live in fear," Wyden said. "For German Jews, the fear was always the knock on the door in the night."[1]

At a 2010 prayer breakfast, he shared with President Barack Obama and colleagues in Congress "a reading from the second book of the Torah, the Book of Exodus," where Moses is instructed by his father-in-law Jethro, a priest of Midian, "on the correct way to govern his people."

Jethro was alarmed at Moses trying to make all the judgments for Israel by himself. "You will surely wear yourself out and these people as well,"

Wyden read aloud. "You shall also seek out from among all of the people capable men who fear God, trustworthy men who spurn ill-gotten gain, set these over them. . . . Have them bring every major dispute to you but let them decide every minor dispute for themselves. Make it easier for yourself by letting them share the burden with you."

The Democratic senator from Oregon continued with the remainder of the story, sharing Moses's success in implementing the delegating proposed by Jethro. "May we all show similar wisdom and be open, open to advice and guidance from any source," he concluded. "Not just within our own group, our own faction, our own tribe, and it is only with that wisdom can we hope to provide just and true leadership."[2]

NOTES

1. Associated Press, "Ron Wyden Says Family's Holocaust Experience Swayed His Thinking on Iran Deal," *Oregonian*, 10 Sep 2015, http://www.oregonlive.com/today/index.ssf/2015/09/ron_wyden_says_familys_holocau.html.
2. *Congressional Record—Senate, Vol. 156, Pt. 8*, 10804, 16 Jun 2010.

Scripture Index

OLD TESTAMENT AND TORAH

New Testament

Theologians and Philosophers

Latter-day Saint Scriptures
(Book of Mormon & Doctrine and Covenants)

Buddhist Writings

Hindu Scriptures

Muslim Writings and Qur'an

Photo Credits

1. John Adams by Asher Brown Durand.
2. John Quincy Adams by George Caleb Bingham.
3. Chester A. Arthur by Charles Milton Bell.
4. Joe Biden, Official White House Photo by David Lienemann.
5. Terry Branstad by Gage Skidmore.
6. Jerry Brown, State of California.
7. Sherrod Brown, United States Congress.
8. Sam Brownback, United States Congress.
9. George H. W. Bush, Official White House Photo.
10. George W. Bush, Official White House Photo by Eric Draper.
11. André Carson, United States Congress.
12. Ben Carson, United States Department of Housing and Urban Development.
13. Jimmy Carter, Department of Defense. Department of the Navy. Naval Photographic Center.
14. Chris Christie, State of New Jersey.
15. Grover Cleveland, Library of Congress.
16. Bill Clinton, Official White House Photo by Bob McNeely.
17. Hillary Clinton, United States Department of State.
18. Jim Clyburn, United States Congress.
19. Calvin Coolidge by Notman Photo Co., Boston, Mass.
20. Ted Cruz, United States Congress.
21. Andrew Cuomo by Pat Arnow.
22. Dwight D. Eisenhower, Official White House Photo.
23. Keith Ellison, United States Congress.
24. Mary Fallin, United States Congress.
25. Jeff Flake, United States Congress.
26. Gerald Ford, Official White House Photo by David Hume Kennerly.
27. Tulsi Gabbard, provided by Tulsi Gabbard.
28. James A. Garfield, Brady-Handy Photograph Collection (Library of Congress).
29. Newt Gingrich by Gage Skidmore.
30. Rudy Giuliani by Gage Skidmore.
31. Al Gore, Executive Office of the President of the United States.
32. Ulysses S. Grant, Brady-Handy Photograph Collection (Library of Congress).
33. Colleen Hanabusa, United States Congress.
34. Warren G. Harding, Harris & Ewing.
35. Kamala Harris, California Attorney General's Office.
36. Benjamin Harrison, Pach Brothers.
37. William Henry Harrison by Albert Gallatin Hoyt.
38. Orrin Hatch, United States Congress.
39. Rutherford B. Hayes by Mathew Brady.
40. Gary Herbert, Wikimedia Commons, 32ATPs.
41. Mazie Hirono, United States Congress.
42. Herbert Hoover, Department of the Interior. Bureau of Reclamation.
43. Mike Huckabee by Greg Skidmore.
44. Andrew Jackson by Thomas Sully.
45. Thomas Jefferson by Rembrandt Peale.
46. Andrew Johnson by Mathew Brady.
47. Hank Johnson, United States Congress.
48. Lyndon B. Johnson by Arnold Newman, White House Press Office (WHPO).
49. Sam Johnson, United States Congress.
50. Tim Kaine, United States Congress.
51. John Kasich, State of Ohio.
52. John F. Kennedy, Official White House Photo by Cecil Stoughton.
53. John Kerry, United States Congress.
54. Dennis Kucinich by Gage Skidmore.
55. Mary Landrieu, United States Congress.
56. Mike Lee, United States Congress.

57. Joe Lieberman, United States Congress.
58. Abraham Lincoln by Alexander Gardner.
59. Mia Love, United States Congress.
60. James Madison by Gilbert Stuart.
61. John McCain, United States Congress.
62. Mitch McConnell, United States Congress.
63. Mike McIntyre, United States Congress.
64. William McKinley, Library of Congress.
65. Richard Nixon, Department of Defense. Department of the Army. Office of the Deputy Chief of Staff for Operations. U.S. Army Audiovisual Center.
66. Barack Obama, Official White House Photo by Pete Souza.
67. Michelle Obama, Official White House Photo by Chuck Kennedy.
68. Martin O'Malley, State of Maryland.
69. Sarah Palin by Greg Skidmore.
70. Rand Paul, United States Congress.
71. Nancy Pelosi, United States Congress.
72. Mike Pence, Official White House Photo by D. Myles Cullen.
73. Rick Perry, United States Department of Energy.
74. Charlie Rangel, United States Congress.
75. Ronald Reagan, White House Photographic Office.
76. Harry Reid, United States Congress.
77. Mitt Romney by Greg Skidmore.
78. Franklin D. Roosevelt by Elias Goldensky.
79. Theodore Roosevelt, Library of Congress.
80. Marco Rubio, United States Congress.
81. Bobby Rush, United States Congress.
82. Paul Ryan, United States Congress.
83. Bernie Sanders, United States Congress.
84. Chuck Schumer, U.S. Senate Photographic Studio/Jeff McEvoy.
85. Tim Scott, United States Congress.
86. Steve Southerland, United States Congress.
87. William Howard Taft, Library of Congress.
88. Zachary Taylor, Maguire of New Orleans.
89. Clarence Thomas by Steve Petteway, Collection of the Supreme Court of the United States.
90. Harry Truman, Edmonston Studio.
91. Donald Trump, Official White House Photo by Shealah Craighead.
92. Melania Trump by Marc Nozell.
93. Harriet Tubman, *The New England Magazine.*
94. Scott Walker by Gage Skidmore.
95. Elizabeth Warren, United States Congress.
96. George Washington by Gilbert Stuart.
97. Allen West, United States Congress.
98. Woodrow Wilson, Harris & Ewing.
99. Frank Wolf, United States Congress.
100. Ron Wyden, United States Congress.

Acknowledgments

I appreciate being raised by parents who taught me at a young age to love the scriptures. My wife, Karyn, has been my partner in rearing our own children, Jessica, Michael, John, and Grace, to love the Word of the Lord. Such passion for God's plan, eternal families, and His comforting voice heard in scripture has led me to this project. The encouragement of family has always been essential in my writing projects, and I forever love them for it!

This book draws on hundreds of sources, from primary sources like speeches and letters, to secondary sources of articles and books. I am indebted to the authors and journalists that have done great work chronicling the relationship of America's leaders with the scriptures, from which I heavily draw. However, I alone take responsibility for any errors in this collection.

The team at Cedar Fort Publishing has been wonderful to give the idea of this compilation wings. Jessica Pettit helped get the ball rolling as acquisitions editor, and Jeff Harvey did a fantastic job capturing the spirit of this book with his cover design. Kaitlin Barwick was extremely helpful as editorial coordinator, and Nicole Terry's editor's eye for detail helped improve the manuscript. Vikki Butler and Trevor Taylor worked hard to launch this book into the world as marketing and sales professionals.

I also sincerely appreciate those who reviewed the manuscript before publishing and shared their generous feedback: Matthew Bowman, Jason Chaffetz, Michael Conklin, Ron Fox, Terry Golway, Bob Lonsberry, Stephen Mansfield, and Beth Silvers.

About the Author

Mike Winder is one of America's experts on the confluence of religion and politics. He is the author of thirteen published books, and his *Presidents and Prophets: The Story of America's Presidents and the LDS Church* was a regional bestseller. His articles on faith and government have appeared in publications from the *Deseret News* to the *Theodore Roosevelt Association Journal*, and he was appointed to two terms on the Utah Board of State History by Governor Jon Huntsman.

He has interviewed Barack Obama, passed notes in church with George W. Bush, sat on the front row of Jimmy Carter's Sunday School class, and talked with Bill Clinton about the president's efforts to help missionaries.

Like his writings, Winder's life has been a blend of religion and politics. He is a current member of the Utah State House of Representatives, has attended two Republican National Conventions, and has been mayor of West Valley City, Utah's second largest city. He is also a seminary graduate, has been an institute of religion instructor, and speaks fluent Mandarin from two years of service as a missionary in Taiwan.

Winder holds an Honors BA in history and an MBA from the University of Utah, and he completed an executive program at Harvard's John F. Kennedy School of Government. He and his wife, Karyn, are the parents of four.

Men: 86
Women: 14

Scan to visit

www.mikewinder.com